# HOW TO TALK BASEBALL

# HOW TO TALK BASEBALL

## by Mike Whiteford
## illustrated by Taylor Jones

Galahad Books • New York

First Galahad Books edition published in 1996.

Galahad Books
A division of Budget Book Service, Inc.
386 Park Avenue South
New York, NY 10016

Galahad Books is a registered trademark of Budget Book Service, Inc.

Published by arrangement with Red Dembner Enterprises Corp.

Library of Congress Catalog Card Number: 86-29164

ISBN: 0-88365-934-4

Printed in the United States of America

# CONTENTS

To Tom Eckel,
who keeps the world
of baseball
at his fingertips

# FOREWORD

**B**aseball is now spoken in several languages, including Japanese, Taiwanese (especially if you're under twelve), Dutch, Italian, and Berra, which means that the late Moe Berg, the most multilingual of all ballplayers and a catcher himself, would be odds-on to be fluent in all five. But Berg's lifetime batting average would probably still be only .243, and while that isn't bad for a spy who parachuted in behind enemy lines during World War II, it isn't too terrific for a man who lasted fifteen seasons in the major leagues. No doubt Berg lasted so long because he knew how to talk baseball.

If you can talk baseball, you can chat with Ronald Reagan, who used to broadcast the Chicago Cubs' games, or to his Democratic nemesis, Tip O'Neill, the Massachusetts congressman who has been a baseball fanatic ever since the time he went to his first game and saw Walter Johnson pitch a no-hitter. In the better part of six decades since then, O'Neill has seen almost everything you can see in baseball except his beloved team, the Boston Red Sox, winning a World Series. At least O'Neill hasn't been waiting as long for his team to win a pennant as Reagan has been waiting for his.

As a matter of fact, if you can talk baseball, you can talk to just about anybody. It is a game that draws together Southern drawls and Brooklyn "dem"s, rich and poor, black and white, clown and counsellor, meaning, in the last case, Danny Kaye and Edward Bennett Williams, both of whom bought baseball teams in recent years. Danny Kaye, judged by some of his scat songs, can probably talk baseball faster than anyone else, and Ed Williams, who defended George Steinbrenner in court (and admitted, in one of the great euphemisms of all times, that some of George's statements were "not in conformity with objective reality") before he became an owner himself, can probably talk baseball more legally than anyone else.

If you have read this far, and followed my drift, you clearly are expert in baseball talk and Stengelian logic. You will enjoy this book. I cannot stop talking without adding my own prime beef with baseball broadcasters: The expression I hate beyond all others is, "He *reached* on a walk . . . he *reached* on an error . . . " Reached *what?*

And one tip: If, after you finish *How to Talk Baseball,* you want to read more, read Ring Lardner's "You Know Me, Al," letters from a busher. It's baseball talk at its purest and best.

DICK SCHAAP

# INTRODUCTION

The first hints of baseball's distinction as a gentle, light-hearted affair emerge long before game time. The players are scattered about, busying themselves in conversation, autograph-signing, playing catch or pepper in front of the dugout or cards in the clubhouse. During BP—batting practice to the uninitiated—the players cluster around the batting cage where laughter and extravagant smiles abound, reflecting the banter that accompanies this pre-game ritual.

By contrast, football players devote their pre-game hours to trying to arouse themselves into frenzied hostility. They pound on lockers and each other. The coaches grimly review the game plan one more time. At a pre-determined moment, often specified by a television director, the players trudge, en masse, from the locker room through a tunnel, ceremoniously onto the field, accompanied by the sounds of bands, cheerleaders, and a raucous crowd.

As game time approaches in baseball, the guys wend their way unhurriedly to their appropriate places on the bench. A more forward player might find a spot slightly to the side of the dugout, making himself more visible to the fans. A crew of relief pitchers and extra catchers shuffles off for the bullpen. At the proper moment the starting nine jog onto the field and stir polite applause among the spectators.

At most ballparks an organist, already having played "Take Me Out to the Ball Game" and other familiar favorites, grinds out the national anthem. Then the game commences, though many of the fans are still settling into their seats or gazing around the ballpark. It's considerably different, of course, at the start of a football game. All 50,000 fans are on their feet screaming. It's tradition, you understand.

Once under way, baseball offers a leisurely, relaxed pace, giving the fans, reporters, broadcasters, and players plenty of time to ponder the proceedings, exercise their imaginations, and allow their minds to wander.

This slow pace has given sportscasters like the Cardinals' Dizzy Dean the freedom to sing "Wabash Cannonball" on the air. Arch McDonald, the old Yankees' and Senators' announcer, used his free time to recite the words to a country ballad: "They Cut Down the Old Pine Tree."

Ernie Harwell, the current Tigers' announcer, fills the intervals by informing his listeners of the fate of foul balls that land in the stands. But Ernie takes liberties. "That foul ball was caught by a youngster from Royal Oak," he says, citing a Detroit suburb. Or he says, "That foul ball was caught by a little lady from Livonia."

The pace may be slow and the action infrequent, but much transpires on a ball diamond to stir the imagination and perhaps give rise to colorful expressions. Look! There's the third baseman sneaking in. He's standing on the edge of the infield grass. He must be suspecting a bunt. But what if the batter swings away and smacks one directly at him? Then third base becomes the hot corner.

A slow roller that dribbles just out of the reach of the shortstop and second baseman seems to have eyes on it. A sharp line drive to right resembles a frozen rope or a clothes line. You could hang out the wash on that one. A drive between the outfielders is a 'tweener. The bat is a wooden implement and is logically called a stick. A good hitter, therefore, is a good stick. An outfielder picks up the ball and fires it to the plate, and his arm is thereby designated a gun. The right fielder has a good gun. A batted ball that travels directly upward, high above home plate, is, well, a home run in an elevator shaft.

Baseball's schedule containing 162 games, not counting pre-season exhibitions and post-season playoffs, contributes in several ways to this fountain of colorful language. Obviously, the six-month grind affords many opportunities for inspiration, and perhaps the monotony of it cries out for a diversion, if only in the form of the spoken word. A 30-year-old man who has been directly involved with fastballs, base hits, and home runs since the age of 10 may want to enliven things slightly by talking of heaters, base knocks and dingers.

The long season gives the sport a built-in safety valve that allows for the daily escape of pressures. It is unlike football where the stress builds for seven days, or tennis and golf where the athletes sometimes await an important tournament for several weeks. And with a 162-game schedule, each game is considerably less important, proportionately, than a football game, which in the National Football League constitutes one-sixteenth of the season. A ballplayer who performs poorly today may console himself with the prospect that things might get better tomorrow.

In its most climactic moment, baseball offers drama, embellished by subtlety and heightened by, say, nine innings and more than two hours of anticipation. The entertainment at football, basketball and hockey games is fast-paced, spectacular and obvious, and often violent, leaving little to the imagination.

Baseball drama is at its best in the late innings, perhaps the eighth, with the score tied or with one team leading by a run. Base-runners dance off first and second, trying to unnerve the pitcher, who peers at them through the corner of his eye. The pitcher then leans in toward home plate, squints and stares interminably as the batter menacingly wig-wags his bat. Finally, after glancing at the runners one more time, the pitcher delivers, the umpire bellows strike two, the entire routine is repeated and the drama continues to build.

The climax comes when the batter reaches out and lofts a lazy humpback liner that eludes the scurrying second baseman and alights softly in the grass—a Texas League single. The runner races home from second and thousands cheer.

Except in rare instances, nothing happens at a baseball game that reaches out and grabs the spectator or shouts at him; it only beckons to him alluringly as he reflects on and considers the possibilities.

Incidentally, the television networks unwittingly mislead their viewers with their 10-second baseball promotions in which an outfielder leaps against the fence to make a great catch, or a base-runner crashes into the catcher. These bits of excitement are entertaining but are highly infrequent and fail to capture the game's essence.

And although it transcends the fans' economic status, baseball contains an element of blue collar that enables baseball to escape the country club inhibitions that sometimes afflict tennis and golf.

In the broadcast booth sportscasters must hold forth with verbal description for three hours a night, six days a week, for six months. And unless colorful expressions and anecdotes emerge, the broadcasts are a tiresome litany of strikes, balls, batting averages, relief pitchers, pinch-hitters, and rehashes of Lefty Longarm's statistics against left-handed hitters in Saturday afternoon games on the road.

An imaginative announcer, however, can add immeasurably to the interest of his broadcasts with an assortment of gems picked up in dugouts and clubhouses. One of the most notable announcers was Bob Prince, for more than 25 years the voice of the Pittsburgh Pirates. An eccentric and talented play-by-play man with a knack for storytelling and catchy phrases, Prince enriched his style with emotion, reveling in Pirate successes and suffering in their failures. Indeed, he openly cheered and exhorted the Pirates, or "the Buccos," as he affectionately called them.

Prince's antithesis is Vin Scully, the veteran Dodger announcer. Scully offers his listeners a masterful re-creation of what's happening down below, supplemented by related information and an occasional anecdote. But his accounts are free of jargon and emotion. He once described himself as simply a reporter and not necessarily a baseball fan.

Because of his popularity, Scully has become a model that younger announcers are emulating, a trend I find unfortunate. The new style, it seems, is to be as forthright as possible, lest the listeners be offended by expressive language, a burst of emotion or the delightful eccentricities of a Prince, a Dean, or a Harry Caray, currently the voice of the Cubs, who is identified with baseball announcing's most famous interjection: "Holy cow!"

Three cheers for expressive language and one loud Bronx cheer for misused language, but I'm afraid the misusers may be gaining on us.

When Dodger pitcher Al Downing experienced the misfortune of going into the record book for throwing the pitch that Hank Aaron hammered over the fence for his 715th career home run to break Babe Ruth's hallowed mark, Downing was asked to comment on the pitch. "I was trying to get it down to him, but I didn't and he hit it good," said Al. "When he picks his pitch, chances are he's going to hit it pretty good."

For a ballplayer to say "I hit it well" would be heretical, grossly out of place in the clubhouse and apparently in violation of some baseball code. And as ballplayers retire and pursue careers in broadcasting, it was inevitable that the word good would be misused over the airwaves.

One such culprit is Cincinnati announcer Joe Nuxhall, an ex-pitcher and still active as the team's batting practice pitcher. Presumably, Nuxhall's pre-game pitches are hit pretty good. This is not to say that the misuse of the word good is confined to ballplayers-turned-announcers. Marty Brennaman, the Reds' No. 1 play-by-play man, is a professional announcer, having learned his trade in the minors before breaking in with the Reds in 1974. But Brennaman obviously has been affected by his exposure to Nuxhall and the players. In a promotional question-and-answer session with the fans of Charleston in February, 1982, he said, "Johnny Bench can play third base as good as Pete Rose, and with a better arm."

Nuxhall's difficulty with the King's English extends beyond his substitution of good for well. He consistently says, "He threw him out easy." Although he brings insight to his broadcasts, his substandard grammar is sometimes jarring and cannot be dismissed as style.

It is significant, and a bit surprising, that baseball language has survived the recent encroachment of high finance. Today's players are contemplating such things as long-term financial security, investments, interest-free loans and lucrative forays into free agency—terminology that hardly seems consistent with frozen ropes, gap shots, 'tweeners, guns, and home runs in elevator shafts.

After playing out his option with the Dodgers at the end of the 1978 season, pitcher Tommy John became a free agent and was looking ahead to his baseball and financial security. And he was sounding very much unlike a ballplayer. "My attorney and I have put together a very attractive package," he said, in the manner of a board chairman.

Although similar references to attorneys are common among ballplayers, it hasn't signaled a shift in speech. Players seem to be clinging to their colorful language and, in fact, are making attempts to expand it and update it without allowing finance to interfere. Apparently, money matters are being left to attorneys.

In 1986, in a conversation with California teammate Wally Joyner, Reggie Jackson referred to home runs as "jacks," thereby converting the longstanding baseball verb "jack"—as in "jack one out of the park"—into a noun. New York Met phenom Dwight Gooden, distinguished for his fastball, also displays an elegant curveball that prompted an interesting alteration of another honorable baseball term. Seeing Gooden throw his curve or "Uncle Charlie," as the pitch is sometimes called, someone decided it deserved a more dignified name and called it "Lord Charles." Someone else saw the superlative curve delivered by California's Mike Witt and named it "Mercedes Bends." Only time will tell whether such expressions will gain immortality.

The players, it seems, are always experimenting with new terminology. In the early '80s, Cubs pitcher Allen Ripley offered an ecology fastball, a pitch that traveled only 55 miles per hour. The Mariners' Richie Zisk once suggested "grenade" as a replacement for the hoary "Texas League single." Zisk must have noticed the trajectory of a grenade throw is the same as that of a Texas Leaguer.

Phillies pitcher Tug McGraw once joked about his shortcomings by inventing the "Peggy Lee fastball," a reference to Miss Lee's song "Is That All There Is?" Kansas City reliever Dan Quisenberry created a sequel: "The Peggy Lee sinker."

The Yankees' Oscar Gamble contributed the "batboy shot," a batted ball obviously destined to leave the park. "I don't even look at it," said Gamble. "I know it's gone. I just turn around and hand my bat to the batboy."

The imaginative works of Ripley, Zisk, McGraw, Quisenberry and Gamble, however, haven't seemed to have gained the widespread acceptance of, say, a can of corn.

In the meantime, it's good to hear the words of a traditionalist, someone who sticks with the old standards—someone like outfielder Dan Ford. Following his trade in January, 1982, from California to Baltimore, he was asked to comment. "I like Memorial Stadium (in Baltimore)," he began. "You can see the ball good. There are big power alleys, and it's short down the line if you can pull the ball."

# HOW TO TALK BASEBALL

# CASEY STENGEL

Though his teams won 10 pennants and 7 world championships during his 12 seasons as manager of the New York Yankees, Charles Dillon Stengel gained greater notoriety for his use of language. Circumlocution was as much a part of Casey Stengel as his bowlegs and furrowed brow. He spoke gibberish and double-talk and was exalted for it. He butchered the pronunciation of his players' names, if he remembered them at all.

At Toots Shor's in New York one night, he was approached by Washington Post sports editor Shirley Povich, who asked Casey about one of his players. An hour later, he was still talking. "But Casey," Povich interrupted, "you haven't answered the question."

"Don't rush me," said Casey.

As central character on the Yankees' glamour teams and embraced by the nation's communications center, Stengel was quite visible, the darling of the baseball writers and broadcasters. He held court before and after each game and seemed to perform better on days when newsmen turned out in large numbers. "My writers," he sometimes said of those who covered the Yankees.

He was a crowd favorite, a familiar squat figure, wearing No. 37, waddling onto the field to raise Cain with an umpire or summon a pitcher from the bullpen. On one of his trips to the mound, his pitcher said, "I'm not tired."

Casey was unimpressed. "Well, I'm tired of you," he said, and beckoned for a new pitcher.

He once compared Yankee second baseman Billy Martin with White Sox second baseman Nellie Fox, saying, "They're very much alike in a lot of similarities."

When the U.S. Senate examined baseball's anti-trust exemption in 1958, Stengel, among others, testified in Washington. In response to serious questions, Casey delivered an assortment of non-understandable patter that even the lawmakers found amusing. Exposed to vintage Stengelese, the Senators repeatedly burst into laughter.

Following are excerpts from his testimony:

**Sen. Estes Kefauver:** Mr. Stengel, you are the manager of the New York Yankees. Will you give us very briefly your background and your views about this legislation?

**Mr. Stengel:** Well, I started in professional ball in 1910. I have been in professional ball, I would say, for 48 years. I have been employed by numerous ballclubs in the majors and in the minor leagues.

I started in the minor leagues with Kansas City. I played as low as Class D ball, which was at Shelbyville, Kentucky, and also Class C ball and Class A ball, and I have advanced in baseball as a ballplayer.

I had many years that I was not so successful as a ballplayer, as it is a game of skill. And then I was no doubt discharged by baseball in which I had to go back to the minor leagues as a manager, and after being in the minor leagues as a manager, I became a major league manager in several cities and was discharged. We call it discharged because there was no question I had to leave. (Laughter.)

And I returned to the minor leagues at Milwaukee, Kansas City, and Oakland, California, and then returned to the major leagues.

In the last 10 years, naturally, in major league baseball with the New York Yankees, the New York Yankees have had tremendous success and while I am not a ballplayer who does the work, I have no doubt worked for a ballclub that is very capable in the office.

I have been up and down the ladder. I know there are some things in baseball 35 to 50 years ago that are better now than they were in those days. In those days, my goodness, you could not transfer a ballclub in the minor leagues, Class D, Class C, Class A ball.

How could you transfer a ballclub when you did not have a highway? How could you transfer a ballclub when the railroads then would take you to a town you got off and then you had to wait up five hours to go to another ballclub?

How could you run baseball then without night ball?

You had to have night ball to improve the proceeds, to pay larger

salaries, and I went to work, the first year I received $135 a month.

I thought that was amazing. I had to put away enough money to go to dental college. I found out it was not better in dentistry. I stayed in baseball.

Any other questions you would like to ask me?

**Sen. Kefauver:** Mr. Stengel, are you prepared to answer particularly why baseball wants this bill passed?

**Stengel:** Well, I would have to say at the present time, I think that baseball has advanced in this respect for the player help. That is an amazing statement for me to make, because you can retire with an annuity at 50 and what organization in America allows you to retire at 50 and receive money?

Now the second thing about baseball that I think is very interesting to the public or to all of us that it is the owner's own fault if he does not improve his club, along with the officials in the ballclub and the players.

Now what causes that?

If I am going to go on the road and we are a traveling ballclub and you know the cost of transportation now—we travel sometimes with three Pullman coaches, the New York Yankees, and I am just a salaried man and do not own stock in the New York Yankees, I found out that in traveling with the New York Yankees on the road and all, that it is the best, and we have broken records in Washington this year, we have broken them in every city but New York and we have lost two clubs that have gone out of the city of New York.

Of course, we have had some bad weather, I would say that they are mad at us in Chicago, we fill the parks.

They have come out to see good material. I will say they are mad at us in Kansas City, but we broke their attendance record.

Now on the road we only get possibly 27 cents. I am not positive of these figures, as I am not an official.

If you go back 15 years or if I owned stock in the club, I would give them to you.

**Sen. Kefauver:** Mr. Stengel, I am not sure that I made my question clear. (Laughter.)

**Mr. Stengel:** Yes, sir. Well, that is all right. I am not sure I am going to answer yours perfectly, either. (Laughter.)

**Sen. Joseph C. O'Mahoney:** How many minor leagues were there in baseball when you began?

**Mr. Stengel:** Well, there were not so many at that time because of this fact: Anybody to go into baseball at that time with the educational schools that we had were small, while you were probably thoroughly educated at school, you had to be—we had only small cities that you could put a team in and they would go defunct.

Why, I remember the first year I was at Kankakee, Illinois, and a bank offered me $550 if I would let them have a little notice. I left there and took a uniform because they owed me two weeks' pay. But I either had to quit but I did not have enough money to go to dental college so I had to go with the manager down to Kentucky.

What happened there was if you got by July, that was the big date. You did not play night ball and you did not play Sundays in half the cities on account of a Sunday observance, so in those days when things were tough, and all of it was, I mean to say, why they just closed up July 4 and there you were sitting there in the depot.

You could go to work some place else, but that was it.

So I got out of Kankakee, Illinois, and I just go there for the visit now. (Laughter.)

**Sen. John A. Carroll:** The question Senator Kefauver asked you was what, in your honest opinion, with your 48 years of experience, is the need for this legislation in view of the fact that baseball has not been subject to anti-trust laws.

**Mr. Stengel:** No.

**Sen. Kefauver:** Thank you, very much, Mr. Stengel. We appreciate your presence here. Mr. Mickey Mantle, will you come around?

Mr. Mantle, do you have any observations with reference to the applicability of the anti-trust laws to baseball?

**Mr. Mantle:** My views are just about the same as Casey's.

On the Huntley-Brinkley report that evening, the final two minutes were devoted to film of Stengel's testimony and David Brinkley could not help laughing as he said good night. Casey Stengel had become a media star.

The 70-year-old Stengel was fired in 1960 following the Yankees' World Series loss to Pittsburgh. It was a move that shocked the baseball world but one that apparently had been planned, regardless of the Series outcome. The Yankees said it was his age. "Most people my age are dead, and you could look it up," Stengel said on many occasions.

When baseball expansion gave birth to the New York Mets in 1962, Casey was the obvious choice as manager. In the beginning, of course, the Mets were awful, but became the best loved and most famous of all inept teams in baseball history, partly because their losing inspired sympathy and partly because of Casey.

At a pre-season press luncheon, he took the floor to discuss his team, player by player, position by position. When he got to right field, however, he failed to mention the player's name, which happened to be Gus Bell, and Casey's circumlocution became more pronounced as he groped for the name. Failing to remember, he shifted to another position and completed the lineup. He then began to make a few general comments. "And we should have a fairly good ballclub," he said, "and we should be ready when the bell rings, and that's the name of my right-fielder, Bell."

His catcher, incidentally, was Chris Cannizzaro (pronounced CAN-izz-Air-o). Casey called him CANS-a-NAIR-o. One of his infielders was Rod Kanehl (pronounced Ka-NEEL). Casey called him Ka-NOU.

The Mets' ineptitude prompted Casey's most famous line, "Can't anybody here play this game?"

Armed Forces Radio Service once invited Casey to interview his catcher, Yogi Berra. The transcript, in part, follows:

**Casey:** I'm awful glad that you've signed. You've been a great success with the Yankee ballclub and for myself as a manager. I wouldn't have been half as successful if you hadn't been a part of it. You and DiMaggio, as I always said, have been my leading players. I can't say that the pitchers were not the same, when you look at what Raschi used to do. Raschi, you could start him in a ballgame and you could be sure to win 4-3 or 3-2. I'd say Reynolds was a tremendous man, starting and relieving, and I thought Lopat was an amazing man, and I don't want to go back to bad times, but you caught all those men, and I'll have to say when you caught Raschi, well, you used to do more of a loving act than I used to see anybody do as a catcher. When you got into a scrape, you would put your arm around him. Now, I thought that looked a little effeminate, but you two must have been very much of buddies.

**Yogi:** Well, that's true, Case. Like I told you before, Raschi pitched better when I got him mad. When he got off the beam, I would go out there and I would say, you're supposed to be a pitcher, and you've been pitching for 15 years, and you can't even get the ball over. And he would get mad at me, he would go right down the other end while I went back to my end. Then we'd make up, though.

**Casey:** Sure, you'd put your arm around him again. Well that was a wonderful thing for the club and I'm glad to hear that you were such a big part of it, and you must have been or we wouldn't have been catchin' you for 14 years and have so many championships with a man behind the plate, because you got big shoulders, Yogi, and you can swing that bat with great success. But, you know, to be a catcher you got to have something over the shoulders, and you got it because you must have a good head because you been doin' that pretty good and because you got a large estate now and—how many was on that boat you was on during the war, anyway? Well, you could put them all in that home of yours if they ever wanted to come and visit.

# RED SMITH

Red Smith was almost universally acknowledged as the nation's best sports writer, a Pulitzer Prize winner who contributed a rare eloquence and wit to the sports pages and who exemplified the notion that sports are a valid part of our culture. "It's no accident that of all the monuments left of the Greco-Roman culture, the biggest is the ballpark, the Colosseum, the Yankee Staduim of ancient times," he wrote. "The man who reports on these games contributes his small bit to the record of his time."

A baseball enthusiast who once traveled with the Phillies and the old Philadelphia A's, Red was informative and entertaining, and had a knack for keeping his baseball writing in perspective.

He once wrote that Happy Chandler was "the greatest baseball commissioner since Judge Landis." Landis was Chandler's immediate predecessor. He commented wryly on the relationship between former Dodgers owner Walter O'Malley and Commissioner Bowie Kuhn. "When O'Malley sends out for coffee," Red wrote, "Bowie Kuhn asks, 'One lump or two?' "

He frequently attacked Kuhn for allowing the World Series to be played in the freezing cold of a late October night and, as a columnist for The New York Times in recent years, seemed to enjoy poking fun at George Steinbrenner's ruthless manner of operating his Yankees. But his disagreements were always professional, never personal.

He wrote not as an expert but as an eloquent spectator at the scene.

His writing had another side. Often, he was inspired to devote his columns to obituaries of interesting sports figures. He agonized over them, as he did with everything he wrote, and they were touching. Not long before his death in January, 1982, those obituaries were compiled and published in a book.

Red Smith was so widely respected for his knowledge of language that he became a consultant for several dictionaries and encyclopedias. To those who asked him how he acquired his literary bent, he modestly replied, "I was a good speller in school."

Because of his writing and reporting skills, he was called upon to cover the presidential political conventions in 1956 and 1968, and he enjoyed doing it. Indeed, he found the conventions closely related to the sports world. "After all," he wrote, "national conventions are games of a sort, and sports offer few spectacles richer in low comedy."

He gained the everlasting devotion of baseball fans by writing the classic reply to those who are forever saying that baseball is a dull game. "Baseball is dull only to those with dull minds," he wrote. He is also remembered for saying, "Writing is easy. I just open a vein and bleed." He thoroughly enjoyed his job, he said, except for those grueling hours spent in front of a typewriter each day.

He recognized and appreciated some of baseball's most elusive charms—its style and subtleties—and, being something of an artist, was able to re-create them with words. In so doing, he helped dispel the persistent myth that good writing does not appear on the sports pages.

# BRANCH RICKEY

The Branch Rickey sentences and speeches that flowered for much of the 20th Century were not always confined to baseball's provincial world. Branch Rickey strayed, extending himself far beyond the game's limited structure, and hit eloquently on an issue of universal importance. Perhaps he was acting as the game's conscience.

"We will never think as a nation," he said, "until the entire nation is permitted to think and act as one." He was speaking of racism, a subject relevant to baseball in 1946 when Rickey employed Jackie Robinson as a ballplayer for the Brooklyn Dodger organization. When preparing Robinson for the inevitable racial abuse, Rickey presented hypothetical situations and warned him to suppress his retaliatory instincts. "I want a player with the courage not to fight back," he told Robinson.

He played down the Robinson signing as simply a measure taken by a general manager to improve his ballclub. "If a man has a woolly face and long pointed ears and yet can play ball like Robinson, I'll sign him without flinching," he said.

Another notion persists, however. As field manager of the Cardinals in the 1920s, he once sat in his Sportsman's Park office in St. Louis and renewed acquaintances with an old friend, a black man he had known at Ohio Wesleyan University. The ballpark's grandstand in those days was not open to blacks, but Rickey assured his friend. "Some day we'll change all that."

A decade after he had integrated baseball, Rickey was speaking out for integration in the public sector. "The single most important issue before the American people today," he said repeatedly, "is eliminating discrimination between the races."

In 1963 at age 81, he was invited to address a gathering of 600 ministers at Lakeside, Ohio. That the ministers had chosen to hear an old baseball executive reflected Rickey's standing as a man of erudition, but

31

his speech was not well-received. "I was contemptuous of the church's role to date in integration," he explained later.

He elaborated: "Ministers, on the whole, are like other people. They want to go slow on integration. They're moderates. In fact, I can think of no major white figure today who isn't a moderate. They call you an extremist if you want integration now—which is the only defensible position. Weren't our American forefathers extremists? . . . All moral people were for abolition a century ago. The Negro then was in rags and chains. He was a slave. How much more important to be assertive now when he is a citizen.

"To advise moderation is like going to a stickup man and saying to him: 'Don't use a gun. That's violent. Why not be a pickpocket instead.' A moderate is a moral pickpocket."

This same eloquence, passion and outspokenness seemed to exhilarate Rickey throughout a career that began at the turn of the century and continued until his death in December, 1965. In his final years he worked as a consultant for the Cardinals, the club for whom he began cultivating pennants in the 30s and 40s.

He relished words, spoke in the thunderous manner of a Daniel Webster and owned a stock of at least 1,000 folksy stories and adages that he employed to enliven his many speeches. "Luck is the residue of design," is a Rickey favorite that emerges today in sports talk.

During his stewardship with the Cardinals, he helped introduce the knothole gang and farm system and thereby contributed a couple of expressions that probably will live forever in the baseball lexicon. And it was Rickey who articulated the five dimensions for measuring a ballplayer: Can he hit, hit with power, run, throw, and field?

His legacy is that of an innovator, a baseball oracle responsible for a wealth of revolutionary ideas, who spread the word, dynamically and lucidly.

He not only originated the farm system but promoted the concept that baseball, being an inexact science, demands quantity, as well as quality, in player development. "Out of quantity comes quality," he was fond of saying.

"The key words are production and duplication. If you have good scouts, and they sign a number of young players, you've got production.

Don't be finicky. Scout with a broom. It stands to reason that if you sign 10 prospects intelligently, you'll be better off than the fellow who signs two, especially in signing young pitchers. They'll fool you."

In his later years, he reflected on his career, noting that he had been educated to be a lawyer, and seemed mystified that his life had been so absorbed in a game. Always expressive, he said, "Imagine, a man trained for law devoting his entire life to something so cosmically unimportant as a game." He held a baseball in his hand. "This symbol. Is it worth a man's whole life?"

# YOGI BERRA

In the dwindling days of a pennant race more than 10 years ago, the New York Mets suffered another defeat and seemed out of contention. But Mets manager Yogi Berra, talking with reporters in his office after the game, was not yet ready to concede.

"It ain't over till it's over," he said, invoking tortured logic to say a glimmer of hope remained. It was a memorable moment—the sports world had made another contribution to the English language.

Of all the Berraisms rushed into print and disseminated over the airwaves in the past 30 years, "It ain't over till it's over" seems to have worked its way most indelibly into the vernacular. Politicians use it to sound bold in addressing problems that appear hopeless. Sportscasters, groping for an appropriate cliche, use it in precisely the same manner that Yogi used it on that historic day in his office. Indeed, the threat of triteness is apparent.

Perhaps the expression someday will merit a spot in Bartlett's Familiar Quotations, a work that presently contains only two contributions from the sports world: Leo Durocher's "Nice guys finish last" and Muhammad Ali's "Float like a butterfly, sting like a bee." Yogi's words deserve to be similarly immortalized.

To be sure, "It ain't over till it's over" is not the best of Berraisms but is the most functional, suited to a variety of occasions, and therefore has acquired the greatest usage. Other Berra expressions that come to mind are equally amusing but, probably because they are less functional, are generally forgotten.

In the days when World Series games were played in the afternoon, the low October sun cast its famous Yankee Stadium shadow in left field much earlier in the game than it did for most of the regular season. Following a particular World Series game, Berra commented on the difference. "It gets late early out there."

When one of their favorite restaurants began attracting too many customers, Yogi and his friends stopped patronizing it, giving rise to another Berraism: "Nobody goes there anymore; it's too crowded." Like most Berraisms, both expressions appear contradictory but, upon close examination, contain valid, if simplistic, observations. Likewise, after the opening game of the 1985 season, Berra, who at the time was manager of the Yankees, told reporters, "I love home openers, whether they're at home or on the road." Yogi simply was saying he enjoyed home openers, whether he was in New York, Boston, or wherever.

It is commonplace for fans and media to perceive Berra, a Hall of Fame catcher and the possessor of assorted World Series records, as a simple and amiable fellow who reads nothing more than comic books and who unconsciously delivers hilarious one-liners that contain a contradictory theme. A caricature therefore has emerged, and the practice of swapping Yogi Berra stories has become a baseball pastime.

Yogi himself says the practice sometimes gets out of hand. In his autobiography, "Yogi," he recalls that someone once told a Yogi story on television. It seems Yogi bumped into a guy who was carrying a grandfather clock and, rubbing his shoulder, told the guy, "For cryin' out loud, why don't you wear a wrist watch like everyone else?" The story is not true, Yogi says in his book, "If I could write lines like that, I'd be working for Bob Hope."

But Yogi occasionally does say things that are quite funny and are, in fact, true. He once said, "You can observe a lot by watching." When he was honored in his hometown of St. Louis, he nervously stepped to the microphone and said, "I'd like to thank everyone for making this night necessary." At lunch a waitress asked him if he wanted french fries with his hamburger. He replied, "OK. But I can't have potatoes. I'm on a diet." He and former Yankee teammate Phil Rizzuto were driving to a banquet and Rizzuto said, "Yogi, we're lost." And Yogi said, "Yeah, but we're making good time."

Sportscaster Joe Garagiola, a lifelong friend who grew up across the street from Berra, invented a Yogi story that he tells at banquets. Yogi, according to Garagiola, once collected three hits in a game, but the next day's paper indicated only two. He then complained to the official scorer. "How come I only got credit for two hits yesterday?" Told by the scorer it

was a typographical error, Yogi said, "What do you mean error? That was a hit."

Yogi knows it's not true but says he doesn't mind. The story, he says, sounds like something he should have said.

# CHARLIE DRESSEN

The situation demanded a pinch-runner, and Senators' Manager Charlie Dressen beckoned to his bench for a player who, as it happens, was a native Cuban who spoke no English. The Cuban took his place at first base and, moments later, a base hit delivered him to third base where Dressen was coaching. Dressen halted the game again and summoned another pinch-runner, an English-speaking one.

This doubtless seemed a bit curious to the Griffith Stadium crowd that included President Eisenhower, but Charlie had an explanation. He wanted someone at third base he could talk to.

Talking was always an important, and sometimes hazardous, element in the career of Charles Walter Dressen, who managed the Reds, Dodgers, Senators, Braves, and Tigers. He is best remembered for a couple of pennants in Brooklyn, as well as for saying, "Hold 'em close, boys, I'll think of something," and a lot of blustery things. Sometimes he stuck his foot in his mouth, or at least in that general vicinity. His chattering was generally harmless but occasionally it was devilish enough to delight reporters and baseball fans.

In 1960 following a two-year absence from managing, he returned as head man of the Milwaukee Braves, prompting club vice president Birdie Tebbetts to comment, "Charlie talks 25 hours a day, but he knows a lot of baseball."

Initially with the Braves, Charlie assumed a dignified air, declining to comment on his managerial acumen or the shortcomings of others, as had been his custom in the previous decade. But before spring training had been completed, the old Charlie emerged.

Would the Braves win the pennant, he was asked.

"I honestly don't know, but write this down," he said, as if the reporters needed prodding. "I'll win as many games as the Braves did last year, and I'll beat the Dodgers."

For Charlie, it was only the beginning. He hinted that the Braves, indeed, would win the pennant, adding that he didn't care what the Dodgers thought.

"If the Dodgers are gonna get mad because I said the Braves will win the pennant, let them," he said. "We got a better team. Let's take Aaron. He's one helluva ballplayer. If you offered him to Los Angeles for Snider, Moon, and Demeter, they'd jump at the deal. And that's their whole outfield."

He then addressed himself to the managerial skills of Fred Haney, the Braves' 1959 manager, suggesting that he was responsible for the team not playing to its potential. "When a team plays for managers who don't teach, what can you expect?"

As a coach for the Dodgers in 1959, Dressen had found it easy to outsmart the Milwaukee manager. "I used to steal his signs all last year," he boasted.

Those given to such outspoken outbursts tend to arouse the opposition and often find themselves with egg on their faces, but Charlie escaped with very little damage. Though they were beaten out by the surprising Pittsburgh Pirates in the 1960 pennant race, the Braves finished ahead of the Dodgers, just as he had said, and the Braves won two more games than the 1959 Milwaukee team, which had tied for the pennant but had lost to the Dodgers in a playoff.

Dressen courted disaster in August of 1953. As manager of the Dodgers, a team running away with the pennant, he surveyed the standings one day and assured the baseball world that those hated New York Giants were no longer a threat. "The Giants is dead," he said. The quotation was enclosed in a box and printed prominently on the sports page of the New York Daily News.

At the time Dressen's words were haunting. Two years earlier, the Giants had trailed Charlie's Dodgers by 13½ games on August 11, but rallied for a miracle finish, climaxed by Bobby Thomson's pennant-winning homer in the playoffs. But there was no miracle in 1953, and Charlie's words were prophetic, if ungrammatical.

The Giants' overtaking of the Dodgers in 1951 demanded some words from Dressen, who responded with enough to match *War and Peace*. Here are a few of those words: "The blunt truth is the Dodgers were over-

rated. They weren't good enough to be out in front by 13½ games in August. They were there because every man except Pafko was hitting over his head, and the second-string pitchers were getting by with stuff that had no license to win . . . . All the guys got hot at once. They were all hitting at the same time. Then, when they got cold, they all got cold. There wasn't anything I could do."

The non-stop talk was transparent to the players, who found Charlie predictable. Just before a clubhouse meeting, a reporter approached pitcher Warren Spahn and asked when the meeting would be about. Spahn explained: "He'll say, 'Listen, you guys. I been here before. I know what it's all about. I been here before.' He'll say that for 10 minutes and that'll be the meeting."

Club officials, too, were resigned to the Dressen style. A Dodger official, reading that the manager had given instruction to pitcher Carl Erskine, sighed and grumbled, "Let's see. He's shown Erskine how to pitch, Duke Snider how to hit and Jackie Robinson how to run the bases. I wonder what he'll do next."

In his career he commented on such diverse topics as the relative intelligence of outfielders and the reliability of former incubator babies. After watching outfielder Carl Furillo strike out three times in a game on the same pitch, Dressen said, "You know, all ballplayers is dumb, but outfielders is the dumbest."

He once learned that one of his pitchers had been an incubator baby. And when the pitcher slumped in August, the manager said, "That's the trouble with incubator babies. They're no good down the stretch."

# RED BARBER

**B**allplayer language has a couple of positive attributes. It is versatile, easily adapted to the world of politics where the politicians forever grope for words easily picked up by the voters. "We're five runs behind in the bottom of the ninth," says the congressman, and we immediately know how bad things are. And some baseball expressions are durable, having existed for a hundred years and are likely to continue for a few more centuries.

But most ballplayer language is generally regarded as frivolous and rarely finds its way into American literature but for a few noteworthy exceptions.

One of these was contributed by Red Barber. While playing poker, the long-time Dodgers' broadcaster picked up the expression, "sitting in the catbird seat" from one of his opponents. He incorporated it into his play-by-play accounts, applying it to a team or player who appeared to be in a highly favorable position. Subsequently, this metaphor not only gained popular acceptance but appeared in James Thurber's classic *Thurber Carnival* as the title of the short story "The Catbird Seat." Barber, too, is mentioned in the story.

In the Thurber story, a mild-mannered accountant, Mr. Martin, contemplates murder because a fellow employee, Mrs. Ulgine Barrows, heckles him with a barrage of silly questions—"Are you lifting the oxcart out of the ditch? Are you tearing up the pea patch? Are you scraping around the bottom of the pickle barrel? Are you sitting in the catbird seat?"

Another of Mr. Martin's fellow employees explains Mrs. Barrows' actions. "She must be a Dodger fan. Red Barber announces the Dodgers games, and he uses these expressions—picked 'em up down South. 'Tearing up the pea patch' meant going on a rampage; 'sitting in the catbird seat' meant sitting pretty, like a batter with three balls and no strikes on him."

The inspiration for the catbird seat began innocently enough when Barber tried to bluff his opponents in a stud poker game. Red had only a pair of eights and nothing in the hole but continually raised the pot, hoping the others would be afraid to continue. He succeeded in scaring all but one to drop out, but the holdout had an ace showing and an ace in the hole and, of course, won the pot.

"Thanks for those raises," he said to Barber. "From the start, I was sitting in the catbird seat." Barber later recounted the incident in Saturday Review. "Inasmuch as I paid for the expression, I began to use it," he explained. "I popularized it and Mr. Thurber took it."

Barber, who announced the Dodger games from 1939 until the team moved to Los Angeles in 1958, also popularized the word rhubarb, giving it a baseball application that means a lively dispute that often results in fisticuffs or a bench-clearing brawl. Its use has spread and the word is now accepted as a synonym for a quarrel.

As he did with catbird seat, Barber picked up rhubarb from an acquaintance and publicized it to his vast audience of Brooklyn fans. He heard it in 1939 from two sports writers, Garry Schumacher and Tom Meany, who, in turn, had heard it from a Brooklyn bartender who used it to describe barroom brawls. Asked why he had chosen the word rhubarb to describe a brawl, the bartender replied that a bowl of rhubarb had always reminded him of an awful mess.

# DIZZY DEAN

**B**ecause of Dizzy Dean's unsettling and ungrammatical chatter as a St. Louis Cardinal play-by-play announcer in 1941, it is not surprising that listeners would raise the subject of syntax. "Sin tax!" Dizzy countered. "Are those jokers in Washington putting a tax on that, too?"

In his heyday as a baseball voice, Dizzy Dean transcended the more conventional limits of America's most cherished and polished announcers—Red Barber, Mel Allen, Arch McDonald, Harry Caray and Ernie Harwell.

Baseball in Dean's era was a bit more colorful than today, and Ol' Diz, of course, was the most colorful of all baseball announcers. Such a distinction did not come easily, considering the presence of announcers like Pittsburgh's outlandish Rosey Rowswell. When a probable home run was on its way over the fence, Rowswell would begin screaming, "Open the window, Aunt Minnie, here she comes!" His assistant, the equally outlandish Bob Prince, would then shatter a glass in the background, and Rosey would say, "Aunt Minnie never made it."

In three decades of radio and television, Dean combined a lovable blend of cornball humor, naturalness, and a disdain for language and convention that eventually endeared him to millions as a result of the nationally televised Game of the Week series that he began in 1955.

He introduced humor to baseball announcing and helped give it a light touch that seemed compatible with the game. And he banished the seriousness that is often the bane of other sports and other announcers.

Dean's appeal was not his broadcasting skill but his personality, his ability simply to talk baseball or about other subjects, related or otherwise, in an incomparable manner. Indeed, he sometimes chose to sing about a Wabash cannonball. Or excusing himself to go to the concession stand for some hamburgers, Dizzy paused to take an order from his partner as millions listened in amusement.

He mispronounced names consistently, abused grammar ferociously and spoke in malapropisms that alarmed those concerned about the possible verbal corruption of the nation's youth. He possessed an intuitive knack for mangling the language artistically and amusingly.

Though English teachers shuddered, Dean delighted his listeners by saying, "He stands confidentially at the plate." After the batter fouled a pitch with runners on base, he would report, "The runners return to their respectable bases." Stan Musial, he sometimes said, "looks mighty hitterish up there." And, naturally, he didn't get Stan's name quite right. It was always "Moozel."

His listeners ascribed such language to his upbringing in rural Arkansas and his lack of education, but Red Barber, the former Dodgers' and Yankees' announcer, suggested that Dean was an intelligent man and that his colorful misuse of English was calculated as part of his style. This same style is practiced today by Archie Bunker, who says such things as "Sodom and Gonorrhea."

A star pitcher with the Cardinals whose career was shortened by an injury, Dean was eventually elected to the Hall of Fame. Immediately on entering the broadcasting field, he began his assault on the English language. He invented his own past tenses, saying, "He slud into third," "He throwed the ball" and "I knowed." He modified the pronunciations of words of two or more syllables, leaving his audience with the enjoyable task of figuring out the correct word. "He nonchallotted that one," he'd say. Or, "He walks disgustilly back to the bench."

Short words were not always safe, either. Umpire was "umparr," and spirit was "spart." Mort Cooper's name was given a hillbilly pronunciation: "Cupper." Marv Throneberry was "Thornberry," and Bill Skowron was "Skarn."

"Don't fail to miss tomorrow's game," he told the fans, and he repeatedly said "ain't."

He once belched on the air, excused himself and explained that it's impolite to belch unless one excuses oneself. "I done excused myself, so let's go," he said.

He indulged in the usual baseball jargon, too. One of his favorites was "can of corn," a fly ball easily within reach of an outfielder.

Most important, his emotion and personality always came through, giv-

ing him greater believability and warmth. Unlike many of his contemporaries and successors, he was not just another placid voice.

When he broadcast St. Louis games, he occasionally referred to one of the Cardinals as "my ol' pal." He exhorted the team from the press box and sometimes bellowed an unkind word down to an umpire.

He was an immediate sensation with the Cardinals, capturing an astonishing 82 percent of the listening audience in his first season, and was just as sensational with his Game of the Week telecasts, which in the beginning were not shown in major-league cities for fear of hurting attendance. But in those places removed from the big leagues, he was enormously popular. Later in his career, the TV blackout was lifted.

Watching Dizzy Dean, it seemed, was almost a religion among millions who enjoyed their baseball embellished with cornball humor and language that was amusingly mutilated.

# DENNIS ECKERSLEY

**H**istorically, Boston Red Sox fans have been a spirited bunch. They're quick to notice the shortcomings of one of their players and quick to castigate him for it. They're just as quick to embrace him for his successes and to exhort him to greater heights.

On a delightful May night at Fenway in 1978, the Red Sox fans were, in effect, embracing Dennis Eckersley, a fellow distinguished for his pitching skills, as well as for his reputation as baseball's leading slang practitioner.

On this night, Eckersley and the Red Sox were leading the woebegone Toronto Blue Jays, 4-0, with two out in the ninth, and the fans were on their feet, stomping, clapping, shouting. They wanted Eckersley to finish with a flourish. They wanted a strikeout.

As it happens, Eckersley induced Dave McKay to bounce out to second base to end the game. Later, in the clubhouse, Eckersley discussed his night's work with reporters.

First, he talked about the fans.

"I knew what they wanted," he began, referring to the crowd's raucous support. "They wanted a punchout. But I didn't want to get caught up in it. I mean it's nice if it happens. But, if I throw him the heater, maybe he juices it out on me."

Next, he discussed his confrontation with McKay, and commented that with two strikes the batter probably had expected the fastball.

"No way he was going to get it. I just gave him a little off-speed job on the outside. He was sitting on my fastball," the pitcher explained.

A newsman's delight, Eckersley expounds at length, immodestly and colorfully, on whatever is happening in his world. New England sports writers quote him verbatim on the assumption that sophisticated Red Sox fans need no translation when he lapses into the vernacular and talks of heaters (fastballs), gas (fastballs), punchouts (strikeouts), juicing it out (hitting a homer), dingers (home runs), nasties (wicked breaking balls), taters (home runs), and taking one deep (hitting a homer), which he uses in various verb forms.

But Eckersley's language embodies more than just the latest slang. In recent years he has been a contributor to the baseball lexicon, either creating his own expressions or picking up obscure ones and popularizing them.

Expressions considered Eckersley originals compose a language known as "Eckese," a term coined by Boston Globe baseball writer Peter Gammons. "Eckese" includes such gems as iron (money), Bogart (opening day), oil (liquor), bridge (home run), take it to the bridge (to hit a home run), paint (a pitcher's control, as in a pitch that brushes the corner of the plate), cheese (fastball), yakker (curve), yak him out (get him out on a curve), hammer (curve), beef (women), and salad hitters (ones easy to get out).

Following a well-pitched game, Eckersley is likely to say, "I had good cheese tonight."

He frequently takes one of his expressions and applies the suffix "master." He then talks of an iron master (a rich person), oil master (one who drinks a lot), and paint master (a good control pitcher).

He describes himself as the "bridge master" because of his tendency to throw home run pitches and teammate Jim Rice as the "iron master" because of his lucrative contract. The Red Sox' 43-year-old Carl Yastrzemski is the "fossil master."

Shortly before the start of the 1980 season, Eckersley had not yet signed his contract and obviously was hoping for a big pay increase. "I want the Bogart because that's where the iron is," he said. To those unschooled in "Eckese," the pitcher was expressing an interest in the opening-day assignment, which carries considerable prestige and usually goes to a highly paid pitcher.

On another occasion, he and Gammons were discussing pitchers Catfish Hunter and Luis Tiant, who had led the American League in surrendering home runs the previous year.

"I'll probably be like them," said Eckersley. "Paint masters are usually the bridge masters." Translation: Control pitchers usually yield the most home runs.

"You take something from everybody you know," he said, in explaining

the origins of his expressions. "Everybody says something funky. But if these expressions had one single originator, it was Pat Dobson (Milwaukee Brewers pitching coach). If you heard him talk, you would think he was my father. I'm not kidding. I learned a lot from him."

For those capable of interpreting it, Eckersley's language seems to brighten his post-game comments to reporters. Observations on such routine matters as sliders and home runs are no longer routine when he discusses them.

Pitching a game at Fenway in 1980, he faced Seattle's dangerous Willie Horton with the bases loaded, two out in the ninth and the Red Sox ahead, 6-2. He promptly fanned Horton on a couple of sliders and then told reporters all about it. "Those last two were real nasties," he said. "In that situation, you gotta go after him. I was trying to punch him out. Can't worry about a tater."

And you can't worry about the wacky lexicon. Somehow the fans will understand.

# BOB PRINCE

**H**is loud wardrobe, kaleidescopic sports jackets matched with Bermuda shorts, and his loud partisan broadcasting on behalf of the Pittsburgh Pirates did not endear him to everyone. His analysis of a Pirate defeat was often interpreted as an alibi. And when he expressed an opinion about a Pirate player or any aspect of the Pirate organization, it was construed as boosterism, and maybe it was.

But when they fired Bob "The Gunner" Prince as voice of the Pittsburgh Pirates following the 1975 season, the Pittsburgh townspeople paraded in his honor through the downtown streets and demanded that he be returned to the air.

Bob Prince never again broadcast the games of his beloved Pirates on a regular basis, although he returned in 1982 as play-by-play man for 20 games televised on cable. But the style he developed in 25 seasons was unmatched in its expressiveness and color. It was a style born of Prince's own expressions as well as many picked up from the players. He forged a colorful and unusual lexicon that surely startled his first-time listeners.

But his radio regulars knew exactly what he meant when he spoke of cow tails, banjo hitters, home runs in elevator shafts, blue darters, frozen ropes, bugs on the rug, cans of corn, wheels, gap shots, alabaster blasters, bloops and blasts and countless others. And if he identified the Pirates as Tiger, Dog, Duck, Cobra, and Quail, his listeners needed no further explanation.

He frequently exhorted Pirate slugger Willie Stargell to "spread some chicken on the Hill," an expression whose origins were traceable to Stargell's early days in the minor leagues and to his later venture into the fried chicken business. As it happens, Stargell had played in a minor-league park where a hill beckoned beyond the right-field fence, inspiring the fans to chant, "On the hill with Will." In Pittsburgh, he owned a fast-food chicken emporium in the city's Hill section and maintained a standing offer of free chicken to every customer in the place at the moment of a Stargell home run.

On one occasion in 1971 when a Stargell homer would have been especially helpful to the Pirates, Prince informed his listeners that he would pay for the chicken. "Spread some chicken on the Hill and send The Gunner the bill," he said.

Stargell promptly homered, and his chicken business was immediately besieged by residents of the low-income neighborhood. They were demanding free chicken and saying, "Send The Gunner the bill." The supply of chicken was soon exhausted, and pieces of paper—IOUs—were handed out to satisfy those who had arrived a bit late.

"They had a riot up there. They had police dogs and everything," Prince explained later. He paid all the bills. They came to $900.

Prince had other, less expensive, methods of pleading for Pirate homers. "Let's have a bloop and a blast," he'd say, meaning a soft single just out of the reach of the infielders followed by a home run. "Let's go downtown," he'd say, suggesting that someone hit a ball to some distant point beyond the fence.

In the Dodgers' early years in Los Angeles, the team played in the Coliseum, where the left-field line was only 250 feet away and home runs were supposed to be limited by a high screen. Well-placed pop flies sometimes dropped over the screen for home runs and therefore were deserving of a new Prince expression. "Let's play a little screen-o," he'd say. And with each Pirate homer, wherever it was hit, he'd say, "Kiss it goodbye."

Prince insists it was he who originated the expression, "How sweet it is," which he voiced mellifluously ("Ohhhh, how sweet it is") following impressive victories. When Jackie Gleason adopted the phrase to open each of his television shows, Prince seemed flattered but reminded his baseball audience of its derivation.

With the advent of artificial grass in modern parks, he updated his lexicon to include an expression appropriate to the carpet-like playing surfaces. A long drive that bounced friskily between the outfielders and rolled to the fence was, to Prince and his audience, a bug on the rug. "We've got a bug loose on the rug," he'd say, animatedly.

In addition to creating his own expressions, he modified a few of the old

standards. A fly ball easily within reach of an outfielder was not necessarily a can of corn, as defined in standard parlance. Instead, it might be a reference to a strain of corn—a No. 1 can of golden bantam perhaps. In Chicago's Wrigley Field one afternoon, he assured his listeners that a Cub fly ball was nothing more than 10,000 pounds of golden bantam for centerfielder Matty Alou, who stood awaiting the ball's descent. But the wind began playing tricks with the ball and, egad, Alou dropped the ball. It cost the Pirates the ballgame.

He coined such phrases as cow tail (to whip the bat at the ball in the manner of a cow using its tail to whip flies off its body), alabaster blaster (a ground ball that bounces sharply, as though off an alabaster or plaster surface) and others with more apparent meanings—as close as fuzz on a tick's ear, as close as a gnat's eyelash and as quiet as a gnat crawling across a bale of cotton. And following a dramatic game in which the Pirates had rallied to achieve an unexpected triumph, it was almost automatic that he would say, "We had 'em all the way."

Indeed, after the Pirates had rallied for five runs in the eighth inning and eventually defeated the New York Yankees, 10-9, in the memorable seventh game of the 1960 World Series, a Pittsburgh newspaper proclaimed in a banner front-page headline: "We Had 'em All the Way."

He was the first to use the term, quail shot, a meekly hit fly ball that travels just beyond the infield and falls quickly to earth for a base hit, duplicating the flight of a quail. Bill Virdon, the man who preceded Alou in center field, hit a lot of quail shots and, of course, was christened Quail by Prince. He originated other nicknames and many of them caught on. Don Hoak was Tiger because of his fierceness, Bob Skinner was Dog because of his dog-like amble, Dick Schofield was Duck because of his walk, and Dave Parker was Cobra because of his style of lashing out at a pitch.

When Prince and sidekick Nellie King—Prince and King—were dismissed, ostensibly for devoting too much air time to matters unrelated to the ballgame and because of declining ratings, they were replaced by an insipid pair of announcers who generally sought to describe the game as forthrightly as possible. They occasionally attempted to be colorful, but lamentably, failed. The lineups, alas, were the menus, and when former Pirate shortstop Tim Foli contributed something heroic, one of the new announcers would exclaim, "Foli Toledo!"

Pirate fans were unhappy with the change, but Prince never returned as the team's everyday radio voice. Later, he spent one season as play-by-play man with the Houston Astros. A former Houston player, Leon Roberts, reported that Prince was not popular among the Astro fans. He said Prince spent too much time reminiscing about his days with the Pirates.

# BILL LEE

The baseball establishment is a stuffy, conservative fellowship that is easily ruffled. It is most vulnerable to a disquieting verbal assault that threatens its image as a fun game played by men who are not supposed to have controversial thoughts and mercenary tendencies.

Paradoxically, the game seems to invite these verbal assaults by its very nature. It's an everyday affair, whose players are accessible to the media in a generally relaxed atmosphere both before and after the game, and its conservatism sometimes elicits unsettling viewpoints from its outspoken players.

And so when Bill Lee revealed to a reporter that he favors sprinkling marijuana on his buckwheat cakes and other health foods, the results were predictable. Commissioner Bowie Kuhn, the bulwark of the establishment, immediately ordered Lee fined $250 and demanded that he send the money to a charity.

Lee's reaction was equally predictable. After sending $251 to an Alaskan mission, he verbally pounced on the commissioner. "If I had sent it to a charity of his choice," he said, "I'm sure it would have gone to Nixon." In an elaboration on the marijuana incident, he used another presidential reference. "Yeh, Bowie Kuhn put on his Eisenhower face and snooped around," he said.

Lee, a moderately successful southpaw for the Red Sox and Expos, is an articulate, iconoclastic liberal, the antithesis of the baseball establishment. If he's not attacking the commissioner, he's saying unkind things about his manager or an opposing manager, or is chastising society for tolerating air pollution. In addition to being controversial, he's witty, thoughtful, and probing. He expounds at length on such subjects as pyramid power, the detriments of sugar, busing, Red China, energy, overpopulation, marijuana laws, and interplanetary creative Zen Buddhism.

These off-the-wall discourses may be spiced with historical, psychological, sociological, and nutritional references. Little wonder that he long ago came to be recognized as the paragon of flakes and space cadets and acquired the nickname, Spaceman, a reference to the drug culture of the late 1960s when the term "spaced out" applied to odd behavior. Lee recognizes his behavior as being different and seems to resent the stereotypical image of today's players. "In baseball, you're supposed to sit on your ass, spit tobacco and nod at stupid things," he said.

"Most players answer questions yes or no," he said on another occasion. "I end up with a two-page dissertation on the Coriolis effect on how the ball spins. I'm not putting people on. I'm telling the truth. But people consider me flaky. The word sinister comes from the Latin for left-hander, you know."

As a Red Sox pitcher, he maintained a bittersweet relationship with the fans, at first endearing himself to them with his fine pitching, later alienating many of them with his views on the city's busing controversy, and finally attracting boos when a shoulder injury lessened his effectiveness.

He defended the Boston judge who ordered desegregration by busing, calling him "the only guy in this town with any guts." And when his pitching skills began diminishing and the boos began cascading down from Fenway Park, he had an opinion, of course. "People started sports to resolve inner conflicts. It keeps them from robbing banks and shooting people."

Other reflections followed the booing. The fans, he said, were too hung up on winning. "I can get off on a really good helmet throw. A connoisseur appreciates that, doesn't boo and watches the game as if it were Nureyev defying gravity."

When the Red Sox sold Bernie Carbo, his best friend, in 1977, he quit the team in protest. When a reporter asked why, he said, "Get some graduate degrees in sociology, economics, and psychology, and then I'll tell you."

He staged a similar walkout as a member of the Montreal Expos in May of 1982 when the team released second baseman Rodney Scott, whom Lee described as a player who "alienated a lot of guys on the team, but I got along all right with him."

The next day Lee, too, was released. And almost immediately he began commenting.

"I'm trying to show that they got rid of me only because I stood up for the underdog," he said. "They are a team that only wants to go for the front-runners. I'm proving to them that they got rid of me because I stick up for my principles."

A sampling of Bill Lee's other verbal offerings covers vast territory.

"I live on the principle that when Julius Caesar was carried into Rome after his triumph, the slave waving the palm keeping the bugs off him whispered into his ear, 'All glory is fleeting.' Everything is temporary. I live in the present."

"My conscience tells me to be a subsistence farmer."

He once called his manager, Don Zimmer, a "gerbil." Later he elaborated. "Gerbils have big puffy cheeks, store food, waddle a lot, and kids love 'em. Zim (Zimmer) and I have a lot in common, but he tries to win at all costs, and I try to enjoy at all costs."

"I heard Jimmy Carter said he has lost control of the U.S. Government. That shows you how dumb he is. He thought he had control to begin with."

"The California Angels couldn't break a chandelier if they held batting practice in a hotel lobby."

"The Yankees are a bunch of vagabonds with bad wheels and a fine sociological study in human frailties."

"Cincinnati's Big Red Machine is about the third best team in fundamentals that I've seen—behind the Taiwan Little Leaguers and the USC NCAA champions in 1968. The Reds act like a drill team; they should be managed by Jack Webb."

"We need alternative forms of living and energy. We need to get into caring for each other and living in harmony with the planet."

When rumors of his imminent release were spreading, he showed up at the ballpark dressed in black. "Nobody looks at me," he said. "They walk by like I've been bitten by a rat from Calcutta, and the disease will spread."

"Baseball players are the people who stay kids the longest."

If he were a football player, he would be absorbed in such things as pre-game growling and post-game exhaustion and thus would be considerably less conspicuous. But the Spaceman inhabits the leisurely and visible world of baseball. And the establishment shudders.

# SHIRLEY POVICH

In the 1920s, the lively and fashionable baseball writers were those who approached the game with respectful reverence, exalting the players as heroes and attaching unrealistic significance to each game. This lofty approach inevitably produced some dreadful language. A pitcher was not simply effective, he threw a "blazing fastball" and had the other team "eating out of the palm of his hand." Teams came "roaring from behind."

To an impressionable young sports writer like Shirley Povich of the Washington Post, such writing was not only acceptable but was an excellent way of doing it. A native of Bar Harbor, Maine, who had idolized baseball players from afar, Povich was easily seduced. In his early years with the Post, he worshipped the ballplayers, as well as the newspaper giants of that era—Grantland Rice, Damon Runyon and Westbrook Pegler.

It was useless, he thought, to emulate Rice, Runyon and Pegler and, instead, he sought to duplicate the style practiced by the Associated Press writers, who treated baseball as though it were the Second Coming and indulged in metaphors so horrid that the memory of them today makes Povich want to upchuck.

At the age of 30 or so, Povich came to recognize that ballplayers were not so heroic after all and that, indeed, some were quite the other way. And as a father for the first time, he realized that baseball was not the most important thing in life.

His writing evolved into elegant and lucid prose, uncluttered by those sickening metaphors, and was irreverent, witty, and satirical enough to reduce a million-dollar ballplayer to more realistic dimensions.

He began his career in 1924, having obtained a job with the Post because as a youngster he had caddied for and befriended the newspaper's owner on a golf course in Maine. He was named sports editor in 1926 at age 21, younger than his colleagues but arousing no resentment. In nearly 60 years with the same newspaper, he lived through the vast changes in baseball writing.

Partly because of his influence, young baseball writers today do not sit in press boxes and use the clichés mentioned earlier.

On the sports pages, baseball players no longer enjoy the deified status they once did. Nowadays their foibles are being written about, sometimes aggravating the normal adversary relationship between player and writer.

And television's immediacy has forced additional changes. "Baseball writing certainly has changed a great deal," said Povich, who favors baseball above all other sports. "It's more interpretive than ever. There's a new school now. No more of just the who, what, when, where and why. There are more personal viewpoints. We have to make allowances for TV. TV covers the hard news, and we in the newspaper trade are writing second-day stories."

To Povich's discerning eye, baseball is a game of intriguing hidden elements that are absorbing to those capable of recognizing them. In his later years, when he no longer covered the Senators regularly, he would attend games occasionally and write lengthy columns devoted to those colorful hidden elements that the game's critics never seem to notice.

"Those interludes in a ballgame that are viewed by some as a bore are, in fact, full of dynamics," he wrote in one of the thousands of columns he produced for the Post. "That pitcher isn't merely fiddling around with the ball in his hand; chances are he is scared to throw it to the big baboon with a bat in his hand who's ready to knock it back down his throat.

"And the batter is not merely knocking dirt out of his spikes. It's probably imaginary dirt anyway. He's just a little bit reluctant to get into the batter's box against that old pro 60 feet, 6 inches away. And when he does, he'll be wondering whether 'the bum is gonna curve me again or try to blow me down with that good fastball.' It's High Noon on almost every pitched ball."

Povich once described these confrontations as romance. "Baseball has more romance than any other sport," he said. He was referring to the dramatic moments in a baseball game that lend themselves to good writing, imaginative prose, and interesting language.

But this imaginative prose and interesting language do not come easily for Povich. Sometimes, he says, he stares so long at a blank sheet of typing paper that he invites snow-blindness.

# PETE ROSE

For the working press, baseball offers an accessibility to the players, managers, and coaches unmatched in other sports. An hour or so before each game, the guys are likely to be seated in the clubhouse or in the dugout or strolling about, available to the media and generally willing to impart baseball wisdom and anecdotes that fans thrive on.

Throughout most of the 1985 season, when he was pursuing Ty Cobb's hit record, Pete Rose's willingness to talk baseball lent itself nicely to America's media-oriented fan. In addition to the dramatic countdown to Cobb, there were the daily interviews in which he addressed the various facets of his pursuit of Cobb's record, as well as countless other baseball topics.

Talking baseball—to the press, teammates, and anyone else—has always been a Pete Rose attribute and has contributed to his popularity and to his image as a man with enormous enthusiasm for the game. In 1985 Rose constantly was chattering away in front of a camera. His picture and comments were always materializing in newspapers and magazines, making him unquestionably the most recognized—and talkative—athlete in this sports-crazed land. For the press and public, listening to him was always a pleasure.

"I've read every baseball book there is, and none of them ever said when a player has to quit," the 44-year-old Rose said in 1985. "I don't drink, I don't smoke. I get my rest and I watch what I eat. In the winter I get up at 7 o'clock in the morning to exercise and stay in shape. I don't know what it is to stay in bed till noon. I make sacrifices, but I enjoy it because I know what it does for me."

Pete approached the Cobb record matter-of-factly, often saying it was simply a question of time. It was not like his 44-game hitting streak in 1978, he said, in which every game brought a new crisis. He was almost nonchalant, though highly cooperative with the media, allowing reporters from Sports Illustrated and Time to spend a night at his home. Even a bit of modesty intervened to temper the famed Rose braggadocio. "I never said I was better than Cobb," he said. "I just have more hits than he does."

When he collected career hit number 4,192 in September of 1985, an announcement of his imminent retirement would have seemed fitting, but Rose dispelled such a notion. "I may play next year," he said, "and I may play the year after that."

His career nearly ended, it seemed, following the 1983 season, almost two years before the hit that broke Cobb's record, but Rose's persuasive skills kept him in the game. Dropped by the Phillies at the end of 1983, Rose shopped around for a new team. He convinced the Expos that his leadership, enthusiasm, and spirit were the ingredients needed to arouse a Montreal team that never seemed to play to its potential.

The Expos took a chance on the 43-year-old veteran, but an injury and a quiet bat kept him on the bench. An unceremonious end to his career seemed inevitable. But in August of 1984, Cincinnati General Manager Bob Howsam looked to Rose to revive the floundering Reds and restore the interest of fans who had been in love with the Reds less than a decade earlier. Howsam, however, wanted Rose as a manager, not a player. Rose, not surprisingly, was not yet ready to retire as a player and suggested that he be a player-manager. Once again, his persuasive powers played a role in his career. "I told Howsam that the people I have the utmost respect for say I still can hit a baseball. Confidence-wise, I never doubted that I could still hit." So Howsam conceded.

In his first game as Reds' player-manager, he demonstrated not only his hitting ability but a flair for the dramatic, a trait expected of great performers. In his first at-bat, he lined an RBI single. Seeing the outfielder misplay the ball, Rose kept running and flopped into second base head-first, a Rose trademark he justifies both scientifically and aesthetically. "The head-first slide is safer and quicker," he once said. "And it usually gets your picture in the paper."

The Reds won that game and compiled a respectable 19-22 record under their new player-manager in the final six weeks of the season. Rose, meanwhile, batted .365 during those six weeks. He broke Cobb's

record in less than a year, a glorious moment in a major-league career that began in 1963.

As a youngster growing up in Cincinnati, Rose was unusually small and apparently lacked the physical abilities essential to success in professional athletics. Yet he sought desperately to succeed, which may explain in part his haste to promote himself with words. "He'd tell you in a second how good he was," recalled Ron Flender, who played in the minor leagues with Rose and who now is a Cincinnati policeman. In the big leagues Rose continued to tell people how good he was and, even as the player with more hits than anyone in the game's history, he occasionally would cite another of his many accomplishments.

In convincing himself and others that he was an outstanding player, Rose probably maximized his abilities and therefore reached greatness befitting the bold. As a manager, he likewise tries to convince his players that they are very, very good. Following his first full season as player-manager, Rose went public to say his right fielder, Dave Parker, should have won the Most Valuable Player Award, that one of his pitchers, Tom Browning, should have been Rookie of the Year, and that his second baseman, Ron Oester, should have won a Gold Glove as the league's best defensive player at his position. Moreover, he predicted that his third baseman, Buddy Bell, would be the league's best in 1986. The prediction was not totally accurate but was close. Similarly, Rose's bold predictions for himself have not always been totally accurate, but have always been close.

# PLAY BALL

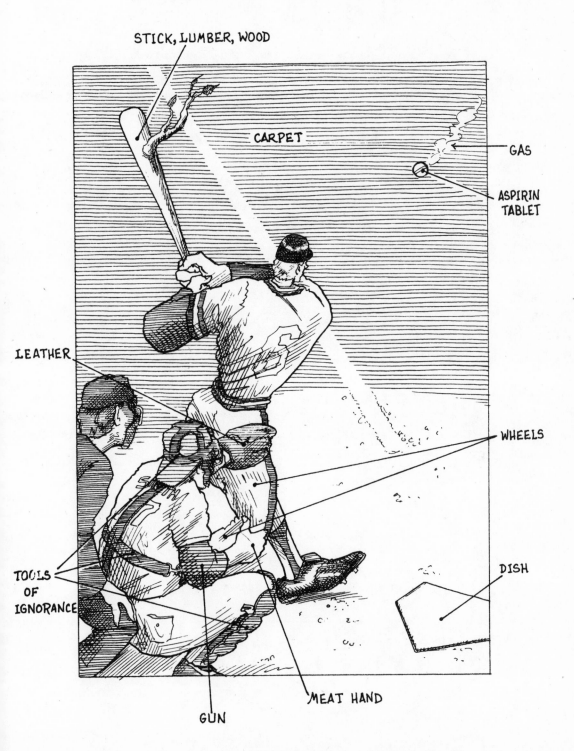

STICK, LUMBER, WOOD

CARPET

GAS

ASPIRIN TABLET

LEATHER

WHEELS

TOOLS OF IGNORANCE

DISH

GUN

MEAT HAND

# Ace

**n:** a team's best pitcher, usually a starting pitcher.

*Tom Seaver*

# airhead

**n:** a dense player, whose head seems to contain nothing but air. Dizzy Dean, considered a bumpkin and a bit of an airhead, once was conked on the noggin by a thrown ball and was removed to the hospital for X-rays. A newspaperman took advantage of the situation in the next day's headline: "X-rays of Dean's head show nothing."

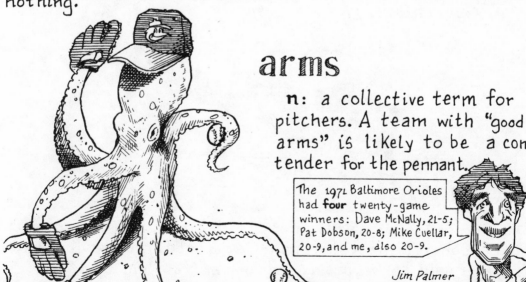

# arms

**n:** a collective term for pitchers. A team with "good arms" is likely to be a contender for the pennant.

The 1971 Baltimore Orioles had **four** twenty-game winners: Dave McNally, 21-5; Pat Dobson, 20-8; Mike Cuellar, 20-9, and me, also 20-9.

*Jim Palmer*

# around the horn

**n**: a double play or an attempted double play in which the third baseman throws to the second baseman, who then throws to the first baseman. It derives from the long trip around the African continent by ship, via the Horn.

# aspirin tablet

**n**: an extremely fast pitch that appears tiny, about the size of an aspirin tablet, as it approaches the plate. Such a pitch also is known as a pill, BB, smoke, heat, heater, gas or one with good velocity.

*Roger Clemens*

# at 'em ball

**n**: a pitch that is hit directly at a fielder. If opposing hitters consistently hit balls at fielders, the fortunate pitcher is said to be possessed of an "at 'em ball." Everything is hit right at them.

# Back through the box

**n:** a term given to a ball batted sharply through the pitcher's box. It usually bounces into centerfield for a base hit.

# bad-ball hitter

*Yogi Berra*

**n:** a hitter who breaks one of baseball's cardinal rules (never swing at a bad ball) by swinging at pitches outside the strike zone but succeeds in hitting the ball well nonetheless. Yogi Berra and Roberto Clemente were excellent bad-ball hitters.

# bad hop

**n:** a ground ball that hits a pebble or flaw in the playing surface and bounces erratically, making it very difficult to field cleanly. One of the most famous bad hops in the game's history occurred in the seventh game of the 1960 World Series with the Yankees leading the Pirates, 7-4 in the eighth inning at Pittsburgh's Forbes Field. After Gino Cimoli opened the Pirate half of the inning with a pinch-hit single, Bill Virdon grounded sharply to shortstop Tony Kubek. A double play seemed imminent, but the

*Tony Kubek*

(bad hop cont'd)

ball took a bad hop and hit Kubek in the throat, forcing him to leave the game. The Pirates took advantage of their good fortune to score five runs, climaxed by Hal Smith's three-run homer, to take a 9-7 lead. They eventually won, 10-9, on Bill Mazeroski's homer in the ninth. A bad-hop single at times has been called "a base on stones."

# ball with  eyes on it

n: a slow roller that narrowly eludes the grasp of at least two fielders as it rolls between them. The ball seems to possess the eyes necessary for such a deft maneuver.

# Baltimore chop

n: a batted ball that hits in front of the plate and bounces high in the air, enabling the runner to reach first base as the infielders helplessly await the ball's descent. The Baltimore Orioles of the 1890's, a team that included Wee Willie Keeler and John McGraw, purposely swung down at pitches in hopes of producing high-bouncing base hits and thus originated the term that is common today. The fact that the Orioles' field was rock hard also helped make this work. Today's Baltimore chops, however, are almost always accidental.

*Wee Willie Keeler*

# band box

**n:** a ballpark whose distances from home plate to the outfield fences are very short, making them easier for home run hitters to reach. The term was derived from the band boxes where musicians entertained the townspeople in the early 1900s. Most modern parks are bigger than their predecessors and do not qualify as band boxes.

Maury Wills

# banjo hitter

**n:** a base hit that results when the batter makes poor contact with a pitch, creating a banjo-like "plunk" noise. Because of the poor contact, the ball is hit weakly and falls just beyond the reach of the infielders and in front of the outfielders. Batters who get a lot of these hits are known as banjo hitters. The Dodgers' Maury Wills was known as a banjo hitter, not only because of his hitting but because he also played a banjo in a nightclub act.

# basket catch

**n:** one made at belt level and close to the body with the glove hand facing up, like a basket. Considered risky and showy, the basket catch was popularized by Willie Mays.

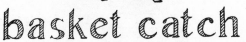

# battery

**n:** the pitcher and catcher, a word borrowed from the military.

# BB

**n:** one of many designations for a pitch thrown so hard it resembles a BB as the batter gets set to swing at it.

# beanball

**n:** an illegal pitch deliberately thrown at a batter's head. The rules now state that if, in the judgment of the umpire, it is intentional, the pitcher will be ejected from the game and fined $50. Bean is a slang term for head that did not originate in baseball. The only player to die after being struck in the head by a pitch was Cleveland's Ray Chapman, who was hit in the temple by the Yankees' Carl Mays on Aug. 17, 1920. After collapsing, Chapman stood up, took two steps toward first, and collapsed again. Use of batting helmets became mandatory in the 1960s.

# bees in the bat

**n:** sting transferred to the hitter's hands as a result of too much vibration in the bat. The vibration is caused by hitting the ball off-center, especially on the handle or toward the end of the bat, and is more noticeable in cold weather. The problem can be alleviated by the wearing of batting gloves.

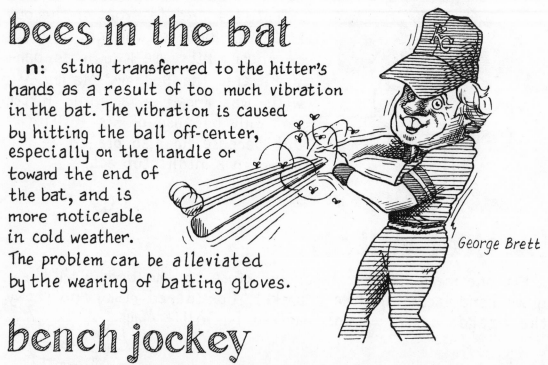

George Brett

# bench jockey

**n:** one who rides or ridicules opposing players and umpires from the safety of the dugout. New York Giants second baseman Eddie Stanky and veteran manager Gene Mauch,

*Eddie Stanky*

STICK IT IN HIS **EAR!**

#⊙!✡☼

(bench jockey cont'd)

formerly with the California Angels, are notable examples. The practice was once common but began diminishing in the 1960s.

# big bill

n: the final hop of a ground ball, named because it bounces to the level of the infielder's cap as he crouches in his fielder's position, where it is easily fielded.

# big show

n: an aspiring minor-leaguer's term for the major leagues.

# bingle

n: a single, usually a modest one.

# bird dog

n: a part-time scout or a baseball enthusiast who points out or helps track down talent for full-time scouts.

# bleachers

n: rows of seats, usually wooden and usually with no back rests where the view isn't the best, and fans exposed to the elements bleach in the sun. The word now applies also to gymnasium seats that have no back rests.

# bleeder

**n:** a cheap base hit. It may be a slow roller that dies halfway down the third base line, a dribbler that finds its way through the infield or a weakly hit pop fly that drops in front of an outfielder. The term is a sarcastic one, suggesting the ball was hit so hard that it's bleeding. Following such a hit, players often say, "Wipe the blood off it."

# bloop, blooper

**n:** a weakly hit fly ball that sounds like "bloop" as it hits the bat and travels just beyond the infield. Bloops take the form of wounded ducks, quail shots, parachutes and Texas League singles.

# blow it past him

**vt:** to throw a fastball that the batter is unable to hit because it goes by him so fast.

Bob Feller

# blue darter

**n:** a low line drive that speeds viciously through the air, as though it were propelled by a blue gas flame.

# boner

**n:** an embarrassing mental mistake, a bonehead play, as if the player's head contained only bone and no brain. The

(boner cont'd)

base-runner who, mistakenly thinking there are two out, runs on a catchable fly ball and thus ends up as the second out of a double play, commits a common boner. Former player Joe Garagiola recalled that, while occupying third base, he once looked up in astonishment to see the runner from second trying to steal third. As the runner slid in, Garagiola said, "Where ya goin'?" The runner said, "Back to second if I can make it." The most famous boner was the work of the Giants' Fred Merkle, a base-runner on first who failed to advance to second following a game-winning hit. Thinking the game was over, Merkle simply walked off the field. The Cubs' Johnny Evers called for the ball and touched second. The umpire called Merkle out, nullifying the run. This boner in 1908 eventually cost the Giants the pennant.

Fred Merkle

# bonus baby

n: a young player, often a teenager who is paid a huge sum to induce him to sign his first professional contract. The term was common in the 50s and early 60s when teams sought to out-bid each other in the pursuit of talent. It virtually disappeared in the 70s with the advent of the baseball draft. A player drafted today must either sign with the team that selected him or wait for the next draft. Draftees today are often paid handsome bonuses, but nothing compared to those of 30 years ago. The Giants' Johnny Antonelli, who received $65,000 in 1948, was a bonus baby of the 50s who justified the cost.

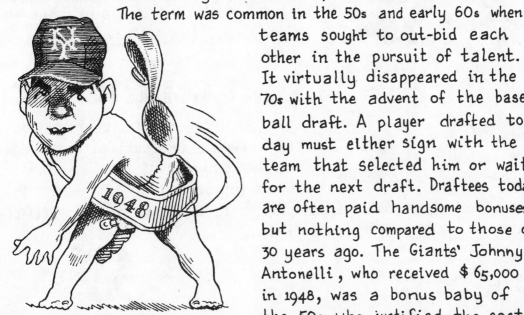

Johnny Antonelli

(bonus baby cont'd)

A celebrated failure was Pittsburgh's Paul Pettit, a pitcher given $100,000 in 1955, who won only one game for the Pirates.

# boot

   n: an error on a ground ball, usually by an infielder, that bounces out of his glove, as though he were kicking or booting it.

# brushback

   n: a pitch intended to move the hitter away from the plate or brush him back. It is not thrown with the purpose of hitting him. Because he threw many brushback pitches when he played for the Dodgers and Giants, Sal Maglie was notorious for giving the hitters a close shave and thus was nicknamed "the Barber."

Sal Maglie

# bug on the rug

   n: a lively hit ball that bounces between the outfielders on the rug-like artificial playing surfaces. It was introduced by Pittsburgh Pirates announcer Bob Prince about 1970 when use of artificial surfaces became more prevalent.

# bullpen

   n: an area adjoining the baseball field where relief

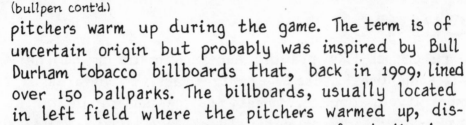

(bullpen cont'd.)

pitchers warm up during the game. The term is of uncertain origin but probably was inspired by Bull Durham tobacco billboards that, back in 1909, lined over 150 ballparks. The billboards, usually located in left field where the pitchers warmed up, displayed a huge picture of a bull. As far back as 1877, the bullpen was the roped-off area of the outfield used for standing room.

# bush

**adj**: lacking class or having the characteristics of a minor-leaguer. A player, manager, ballpark, or town may be described as bush league. The term comes from one meaning of the word bush-- common, uncultivated.

# Cactus League

**n**: the teams that locate in Arizona for spring training and comprise an exhibition-game circuit. The Angels train in Palm Springs, Calif., but compete in the Cactus League.

# can of corn

**n**: a fly ball within easy reach of an outfielder. "It's as easy as taking corn out of a can," said Pirates announcer Bob Prince, who used the expression often.

# can't miss

**adj**: having the youth and skills that portend stardom.

# carpet

n: carpet-like playing surfaces made of synthetic material, sometimes called ersatz grass. It affords a truer but more lively bounce, sometimes resulting in balls bouncing over the heads of outfielders, a situation that usually does not happen on natural grass.

# carry

n, vi: the distance of a fly ball, which depends not only on how hard the ball is hit but on wind, air density, and humidity. Carry varies from day to day and from ballpark to ballpark.

# catch him leaning

vt: to pick a runner off base, usually first, as he takes his lead and leans toward the next base in anticipation of either stealing or getting a good start.

Rickey Henderson

# caught looking

vi: to be fooled by a pitch that crosses the plate for a called third strike. In describing such pitches, former Yankees and Senators announcer Arch McDonald would say it was "right down Broadway"

Ray Knight

# chatter

n: lively talk among infielders on the field designed to encourage the pitcher and keep everyone alert. The practice is

(chatter cont'd.)

not as common as it once was. One of the most enthusiastic practitioners today was Mets' third baseman Ray Knight.

# chin music

n: a knockdown pitch, one that comes perilously close to the batter's chin. Because of baseball's rules against knockdown pitches, chin music is not as common as it was during the 50s when pitchers were likely to brush back a hitter who was too aggressive. The Dodgers' Don Drysdale was well-versed in chin music. Once, after surrendering a couple of home runs to Hank Aaron, Drysdale threw a pitch that hit Hank in the back. The next day in batting practice, Drysdale supposedly yelled, "Sorry I hit you in the back yesterday, Hank." Hank responded politely that it was OK. And Drysdale said, "I meant to hit you in the neck."

# choke hitter

n: one who grips the bat several inches from the bottom, thus creating the impression that he is grabbing it by the neck and "choking" it. Choke hitters sacrifice power for control.

# circus catch

*Willie Mays*

n: a spectacular catch; one that requires an extraordinary effort. Originally, it was a negative term applied to players who were trying to show off for the fans by making routine plays seem more difficult. It was as if they were performing at a circus. Today, the term no longer carries a negative connotation. It first appeared before the turn of the century.

*Dick Stuart*

# clang

**n**: a bad fielder, whose hands seem to be made of iron and who, figuratively, makes a clanging noise when the ball bounces off his glove. Such players are also known as iron hands and iron glove. In 1963, Boston's bad-fielding first baseman Dick Stuart was nicknamed Dr. Strangeglove shortly after the release of the movie *"Dr. Strangelove."* Once when Stuart earlier played for the Pittsburgh Pirates and when public address announcer Art McKennan made his traditional first-inning announcement, "Anyone interfering with a ball in play will be ejected from the ballpark," Pirate Manager Danny Murtaugh turned to the players on the bench and said, "I hope Stuart doesn't think that means him."

# cleanup

**adj**: the No. 4 position in the batting order, a position usually filled by a power hitter whose job is to clean up the bases, that is, to get a hit so that the runners will score. Hank Aaron and Lou Gehrig were the most famous of baseball's cleanup men and rank second and third, respectively, in career RBIs. The leading RBI man was Babe Ruth, who generally batted third.

*Hank Aaron*

# closed stance

**n**: the positioning of the batter's feet in which the front foot is closer to the plate than the back foot.

# clothes line

**n:** a hard hit low line drive that travels as straight as a clothes line.

# clubhouse lawyer

**n:** a player who is often expressing his radical or reform-minded opinions about baseball to other players, usually in the clubhouse. Because the Major League Players Association has assured today's players of favorable travel conditions and meal money, frequent off-days, a generous retirement plan and other perquisites, clubhouse lawyers are not as common as they were 20 years ago. Players are more content today and find less reason to seek reform.

*Wade Boggs*

# clutch

**adj:** a time in the game where a player has to make a crucial play. It may apply to any facet of the game--hitting, pitching, base-running or defense.

# collar

**n:** a designation that signifies that a batter went without a hit for a particular game. A batter without a hit "wears the collar."

# come-backer

**n:** a ball batted directly back to the pitcher.

Steve Carlton

Johnny Bench

# cousin

n: a team or pitcher that unexplainably is an easy mark for another team or hitter. A team (or pitcher) may be a cousin to one team but a nemesis to another. Kansas City was Baltimore's cousin from May, 1969, to August, 1970, during which time the Orioles defeated the Royals 23 consecutive times. Steve Carlton, doubtless a future Hall of Famer, has been a cousin to the Reds, who have beaten him in 18 of 29 decisions.

# cripple

n: a pitch thrown with three balls, no strikes or three balls, one strike in which the pitcher must throw the ball in the strike zone if he is to avoid giving up a walk. Thus, the pitcher often throws with less speed to try to get more control, and the pitch arrives slightly "crippled."

# cup of coffee

n: a very brief stint in the major leagues. A player who is promoted to the majors but who is returned to the minors in a few weeks is said to have been up "for a cup of coffee." This often happens in September when big-league teams are allowed to expand their rosters beyond the 25-player limit.

# Delayed double steal

n: a play in which, with runners at first and third, the man at first base breaks for second in an attempt to steal. If the catcher throws to second, the man at third may gamble and try to steal home and, if successful, has executed the scoring half of a delayed double steal. Sometimes, the catcher bluffs a throw to second and throws instead to third, hoping to catch the runner off base.

# delivery

n: a pitch or the act of throwing a pitch, i.e., a pitcher's windup and follow-through.

# deuce

n: a curve, derived from the custom of catchers' holding down two fingers to signify the pitcher to throw a curve.

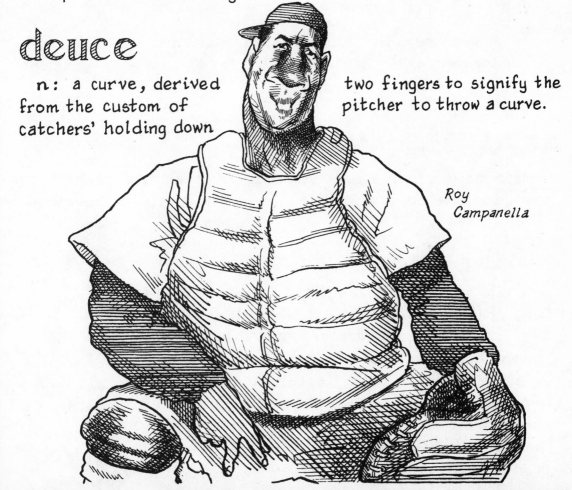

Roy Campanella

# dial 8

vi: to hit a home run, as in dialing 8 on a hotel phone for long distance.

# dinger

n: a home run.

# dish

n: home plate.

*Jim Rice*

# dome dong

n: a home run in a domed stadium, a phrase first applied to homers in Seattle's Kingdome, whose dimensions favor power hitters.

# downtown

n: a home run, a ball hit out of the park perhaps en route to some point downtown. To homer is to go "downtown."

# drag bunt

n: if perfectly executed, a drag bunt rolls along the first-base line, as if it were being dragged by the runner going to first. A drag bunt can be attempted only by a left-hander, who actually takes a step toward first before bunting the ball. Because of his speed, Mickey Mantle was a talented drag bunter in his early seasons.

*Mickey Mantle*

# ducks on the pond

**n:** runners on base waiting to be driven home. Coined by Arch McDonald, the former Senators and Yankees announcer. It was Arch McDonald who in 1939 gave Joe DiMaggio his famous nickname of "The Yankee Clipper," which was a swift Boston-to-New York train.

# duster

**n:** an inside pitch thrown to make the batter jump away from the plate, sometimes causing him to tumble backwards into the dirt. When Minnesota pitcher Ron Davis was accused of throwing at Detroit hitters, he explained: "When it (the pitch) does get away from me, it's high and tight. I was never trying to dust anybody." Dusters and brushbacks are intended only to come close to the hitter and are not the same as beanballs.

# Eephus

**n:** a pitch that is thrown on a high arc to a height of about 10 to 12 feet off the ground and is supposed to drop into the strike zone. It was invented by Pittsburgh's Rip Sewell in the 1940s and given its name by teammate Maurice Van Robays. The pitch is more commonly called a blooper ball. Veteran pitcher Dave LaRoche, who pitches for the Yankees and their triple-A farm club, throws the pitch and has christened it the "LaLob."

*Rip Sewell*

# Fan

*Dale Murphy*

**vi, vt:** to strike out, as in fanning the breeze. As a noun, fan is the most common word to identify an enthusiastic spectator. Its origin is unclear. One theory is that it is a derivative of "fanatic." Another is that it was borrowed from the British word "fancy," which originally meant a boxing enthusiast and was later shortened to "fance" and "fans." Long~time Philadelphia A's Manager Connie Mack suggested that spectators were called "fans" because they fanned themselves in hot weather.

*Branch Rickey*

# farm

**n:** minor-league teams whose purpose is to develop talent for the major-league club that either owns them or maintains a working agreement with them. The practice of selling or assigning major-league players to minor-league teams began in 1887, and the term "farming out" was first used at about the same time. The minor leagues reached a peak in 1949 when there were 59 leagues and 450 teams. In 1981, largely because of television, there were only 17 leagues and 154 teams. Minor-league teams were independent until the 1920s when St. Louis Cardinals executive Branch Rickey introduced the farm system. Because it proved beneficial to the Cardinals, other teams began developing farm systems.

# field general

**n:** a stilted term for manager.

John McGraw

# fireman

**n:** a relief pitcher who specializes in entering the game in the midst of a late-inning hot situation when the opposing team is threatening to score to douse the fire. He is also known as a short reliever because he rarely pitches more than three innings at a time. The all-time leading fireman is Rollie Fingers, who had 272 career saves through the 1981 season. Two of the early firemen were the Yankees' Joe Page and the Dodgers' Hugh Casey, who pitched in the late 40s and early 50s. Page had 76 saves and Casey 55. Pirate fireman El Roy Face compiled an 18-1 record in 1959. Saves were not a part of baseball's statistical world in the era of Page, Casey and Face. Saves for pitchers back then were compiled by researchers poring over 30-year-old score sheets.

Rollie Fingers

# flake

**n:** a player who talks or acts eccentrically. Bill Lee gained special flake status by wearing a gas mask to the ballpark to protest air pollution. Jimmy Piersall once homered and circled the bases running backwards. On another occasion he wore a Beatle wig. Pitcher Mark Fidrych talked to the ball, dropped to his hands and knees to re-arrange the dirt on the mound and, in the middle of an

The Bird

(flake cont'd)

inning, shook hands with infielders who had made outstanding plays. As a player for the Giants in the 1920s, Casey Stengel doffed his cap to the fans and a bird flew out. Rick Dempsey entertained the crowd during rain delays by running onto the tarp and sliding head-first through puddles.

# foot in the bucket

**n:** a derisive term for a batting style in which the hitter moves his front foot sideways, away from the plate as he swings at the ball. A right-handed batter facing a side-armed right-handed pitcher is more likely to do so. The expression first appeared in the days when drinking water was kept in buckets in the dugouts. A hitter moving his front foot away from the plate seemed to be stepping toward the dugout, as if "spiking the water bucket." Hall of Famer Al Simmons batted with his foot in the bucket and was known as Bucketfoot. Roy Campanella and Arky Vaughan also were outstanding foot in the bucket hitters.

Al Simmons

# free ticket

**n:** a base on balls.

# frozen rope

**n:** a sharply hit ball (it may or may not drop for a hit) that travels low to the ground and follows a path as straight as a frozen rope. It is indistinguishable from a rope, clothes line, blue darter and a screaming meemie.

# fungo

n: a long, thin bat used by a coach or player who tosses balls in the air and hits flies and grounders during practice sessions. A ball hit in such a manner also is known as a fungo.

# Gamer

n: an intense, resolute player willing to play in pain and under adverse conditions. He's game for anything. On July 15, 1967, St. Louis pitcher Bob Gibson was struck in the leg by a line drive off the bat of Pittsburgh's Roberto Clemente. He continued to pitch but later discovered his leg was broken.

Bob Gibson

# gap

n: the area between the left-and-centerfielders or the center-and-rightfielders. Gap, however, does not apply to the area between infielders.

# gap shot

n: an extra-base hit that lands in the gap between two outfielders and scoots past them and generally rolls to the wall.

# gas

n: one of many synonyms for fastball that are related to the heat generated by a rapidly moving object. (See heat)

# glove man

n: a good fielder, often one who is not a good hitter.

# goat

n: a derivative of scapegoat, a player blamed for a defeat because of his error or mistake. In Biblical times, a scapegoat was a goat exiled to the wilderness, symbolically bearing the sins of others. One of baseball's most noted goats was Fred Snodgrass, a New York Giants centerfielder, who dropped an easy fly ball, contributing to Boston's tying and winning runs in the seventh game of the 1912 World Series.

Bill Mazeroski, who holds many major league fielding records, also hit the winning home run of the 1960 World Series against the Yankees.

Bill Mazeroski

# gopher ball

n: a pitched ball that is hit for extra bases, usually a home run. In 1938, Ken Ohst of WHA Radio in Madison, Wis., asked the Yankees' Lefty Gomez about "gopher ball." Said Lefty: "It's an errant pitch that will sometimes "gofer" a double, sometimes "gofer" a triple, and sometimes "gofer" a home run.

# grand slam

n: a home run with the bases loaded, a phrase borrowed from bridge where it refers to a scoring unit. The linguistic switch from bridge to baseball was facilitated by the fact that slam also carries a hitting connotation.

# Grapefruit League

n: the teams that locate in Florida for spring training and comprise an exhibition-game circuit. The practice of professional teams going south for

(Grapefruit League cont'd.)

pre-season training was originated by the Chicago White Stockings, who traveled to New Orleans in 1870.

# green light

**n:** a signal from the third base coach that gives the batter the freedom to swing at the next pitch. Hitters are sometimes given the "take sign," which forbids them from swinging at the next pitch.

*Tris Speaker*

# gun

**n:** the name given to an outstanding throwing arm of a fielder, particularly an outfielder. Strong-armed outfielders sometimes have inspired gun-related nicknames. Carl Furillo of the Dodgers was called the Reading Rifle because of his minor-league playing days in Reading, Pa., and George Shuba, also of the Dodgers, was known alliteratively as Shotgun Shuba. The record for most outfield assists is owned by Hall of Famer Tris Speaker, who threw out 449 runners in his 22 seasons. The single-season record is 44 by Chuck Klein of the Phillies in 1930.

# gun-shy

**adj:** being afraid of the ball, either as a hitter or fielder. A player injured by a pitched ball is sometimes gun-shy in his next few at-bats.

# Handcuffed ⚾

**adj, adv**: to be unable to handle a hard hit ground ball or one that takes a nasty hop. An infielder handcuffed is said to be "eaten up" by a ground ball. Though they're hit directly at him, ground balls that handcuff a player are sometimes scored as base hits.

# handle

**n**: a fielder's ability to get a firm grip on the ball. One who errs is often one who "can't find the handle."

# hanging curve

**n**: an improperly thrown curve that fails to break sharply as a good curve is supposed to do. Instead, it either travels straight, all the while spinning but not breaking, or curves lazily on a flat plane. A bane to all pitchers, the hanging curve is a hitter's delight and is an easy home run target for even poor hitters.

Don Drysdale

# headhunter

**n**: a derisive word for a pitcher who supposedly throws at hitters, specifically at their heads.

# heat, heater

**n**: an exceptionally good fastball. A reference to the friction generated by a rapidly moving object, heat and heater are among the game's most widely used expressions. Other words for heat are smoke, blazer, gas and high octane. Players often speak of high gas and low gas, depending on the pitch's

(heat, heater cont'd)

location. A legendary generator of heat was a pitcher who never made it to the majors and who was only 5-foot-9 and weighed 160 pounds. He was Steve Dalkowski, who played in the Baltimore organization in the late 1950s and who, according to Oriole Manager Earl Weaver, threw harder than anyone in the past 25 years. In Class D one year, he struck out 121, walked 129 and threw 39 wild pitches in 62 innings.

Jack Morris

# heavy ball

n: a ball thrown in such a manner and with a degree of spin that it feels heavy, and often painful, to the player catching it. Catchers say that handling an 85 mph heavy ball is considerably tougher on the hand than a 100 mph light ball. Pitchers known for throwing heavy balls are Mel Stottlemyre, Steve Blass and Goose Gossage.

# high, hard one

n: an overpowering fastball high in the strike zone.

# hill

n: the pitcher's mound.

# hit-and-run

n: a play in which the runner breaks for second base, as though stealing, and the batter is obligated to hit the ball to protect the runner. A perfectly executed hit-and-run is one in which the runner breaks for second and, as either the second baseman or shortstop moves to cover the base, the batter strokes a base hit to the area vacated by the infielder. The base-runner then usually makes third base easily. The Dodgers' Gil Hodges, who later managed the Senators and Mets, described the Giants' Alvin Dark and the Pirates' Dick Groat as the two best hit-and-run hitters of his era.

# hitch in his swing

n: a bad habit in which the batter drops his hands suddenly just before he swings at a pitch, and this usually disrupts his timing.

# hit for the cycle

vt: one of baseball's rarest feats, where a batter gets a single, double, triple and home run in one game. Babe Herman, who played for the Dodgers and Cubs, and Bob Meusel, who played for the Yankees, are the only players in baseball history to perform the feat three times in a career.

# home run in an elevator shaft

n: a ball batted straight up and especially high. An imaginative fan may want to set his own guidelines as to what qualifies as an elevator shaft homer—perhaps a ball that stays within

Reggie Jackson

(home run in an elevator shaft cont'd)

a 15-foot radius of home plate.

# hook

**n:** one of many designations for a curve ball, originated because a hook resembles the path of a curve.

# Hoover

**n:** a skillful infielder who fields or sweeps up ground balls as though he were a Hoover vacuum.

# horsehide

**n:** the baseball. Balls are covered with either horsehide or cowhide.

*Brooks Robinson,*
*Hoover in the hot corner*

# hot corner

**n:** the third base position, a common expression that refers to the frequency of hot line drives and grounders that assault the third baseman, who is 90 feet from the hitter. The term originated in the 1880s when a sports writer wrote that a series of hard-hit balls had the third baseman "on the hot corner all afternoon."

# hot dog

**n:** a player whose actions are calculated to draw attention to himself. The term is not necessarily one of derision. The hot doggery of a popular player is interpreted as zest or good showmanship. Part of Pete Rose's appeal is that he slides head~first into a base, regardless of whether a play is being made on him. Willie Mays cleverly disguised his acts of hot doggery. When running the bases or pursuing a fly ball, he often ran out from under his cap, a circumstance the fans quickly noticed and found entertaining. Willie later admitted that he adjusted his cap a bit loosely to ensure that it would fly off at an opportune moment. In his early years with the Yankees, a brash Babe Ruth was full of himself. He strode slowly and deliberately to the plate and stood outside the batter's box, unleashing a barrage of ferocious swings. He was aware of his celebrity status and played to the crowd, though the term hot dog was not in vogue at the time. In the late 1940s and 50s, Cuban players began to call each other hot dogs and the expression spread.

*Pete Rose*

# hot stove league

**n:** mid-winter talk among fans to pass the time while eagerly anticipating the new season. It's an allusion to cartoonists' favorite scene of a group of fans huddled around an old~fashioned stove talking baseball.

# hummer

**n:** one of many synonyms for fastball, named because of the humming sound produced by the ball rocketing toward the plate

# hump~back liner

**n:** a cross between a frozen rope and a parachute. The ball is hit with moderate power, rises to an altitude of about 20 feet and falls to earth in front of the outfielders.

# Intensity

**n:** a fashionable sports word applied to players who combine determination and concentration.

Dave Stieb

# in the hole

**prep. phrase:** an area deep in the infield and far to the right of the shortstop. If a shortstop succeeds in fielding a ball deep in the hole, he will have more difficulty throwing out the runner because of the longer distance to first base.

# Jack

**vt:** to hit the ball a great distance. "He jacked one."

# jam

**n:** a difficult situation for the team in the field as "in a jam." Perhaps the bases are loaded and nobody out. Also it

(jam cont'd)

means to pitch close to a batter, usually on the inside corner of the plate so the batter gets only a cramped swing at the ball. If Yankee Manager Casey Stengel wanted his pitchers to jam the hitters, he told them to "find their pots and pans." When the opposition pitched close to Boston's George Scott, he described it as "pitchin' to my kitchen."

# journeyman

n: a well-traveled, veteran ballplayer who has bounced around from team to team during his career. The player with the record for having played for the most teams is Dick Littlefield. Between 1950 and 1958, he played for 10 clubs -- the Red Sox, White Sox, Tigers, Browns, Orioles, Pirates, Cardinals, Giants, Cubs, and Milwaukee Braves.

*Dick Littlefield*

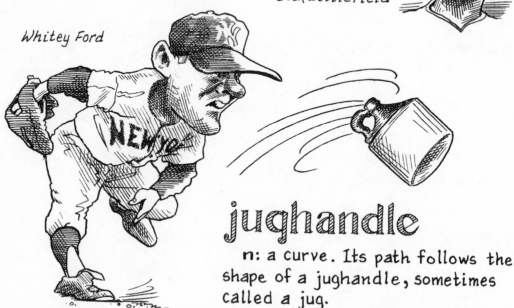

*Whitey Ford*

# jughandle

n: a curve. Its path follows the shape of a jughandle, sometimes called a jug.

# juice

vt: to hit the ball a long way, usually for a home run, thus generating plenty of power. A player "juices one" or "juices one out."

# jump

**n:** a base-runner's lead, how far he positions himself off the base, and the quickness of his start in a stolen base attempt. A player getting a good jump on the pitcher is likely to steal a base.

# junk

**n:** a pitcher's assortment of softly thrown pitches that includes only breaking balls, off-speed deliveries or Knuckleballs. The Yankees' Eddie Lopat was one of the better junk specialists.

*Eddie Lopat*

# K

**n:** a symbol that designates a strikeout, when keeping a scorecard. First used in the 1860s, it was chosen because it is the last letter in the word struck, and it avoided confusion with "S" that has always stood for sacrifice. "KS" means a swinging strikeout, "KC" means a called strikeout and "K 2-3" means a strikeout in which the catcher drops the ball and must pick it up and throw to first to complete the out.

## ~THE DIAMOND~

Fans and media people who keep a scorecard use numbers as simple designations for fielders. If, for example, the shortstop picks up a ground ball and throws to first, the entry in the scorecard would read 6-3

**8** Centerfielder
**7** Leftfielder
**9** Rightfielder
**6** Shortstop
**4** Second Baseman
Third Baseman **5**
Pitcher **1**
**3** First Baseman
90'
90'
90'
90'
60'6"
**2** Catcher

# keystone

**n:** second base, given the name because, like the architectural keystone, it is a vital area when well-covered by second basemen and shortstops that results in a good defensive infield. Double play combinations are sometimes called keystone combinations.

# knothole gang

**n:** a ballpark admissions plan in which youngsters and youth baseball teams, often in full uniform, are admitted to games free or at greatly reduced prices. A Saturday afternoon is usually designated as Knothole Day. The idea was popularized by Branch Rickey, general manager of the Cardinals, in the 1930s. The image of kids watching a ballgame through a knothole in the fence was the inspiration for the name.

# Ladies' day

**n:** the promotional custom of admitting women free or for a small charge plus tax. The St. Louis Browns helped establish ladies' day in 1912. At first, the Browns required that women must have escorts but dropped the provision when females began congregating in front of the park, looking for escorts. The Cincinnati Red Stockings originated a type of ladies' day before the turn of the century. When he noticed that women were

(ladies' day cont'd)

especially numerous on days that a particularly handsome Cincinnati pitcher was on the mound, the team owner advertised that this fellow would pitch every Monday and that all women accompanied by an escort would be admitted free.

# laugher

n: the winning team's expression for an easy, one-sided victory. The losing team dismisses it as "one of those days."

*Tim Raines*

# leadoff

n: the first position in the batting order, usually manned by a player who hits well but is generally a singles hitter, has a knack for drawing walks, and runs the bases well. The Yankees' Rickey Henderson and the Expos' Tim Raines are two of the best leadoff men of all time because of their ability to reach base and steal.

# leather

n: a glove or an all-purpose word for fielding. A good fielder is one with "a lot of leather."

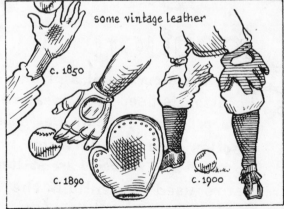

some vintage leather

c. 1850

c. 1890

c. 1900

# leg hitter

n: a speedster adept at getting on base by beating out slow rollers and bunts. Pittsburgh's Lloyd (Little Poison) Waner made good use of leg hits to set a record of 198 singles in 1927. Kansas City's Willie Wilson, Cleveland's Miguel Dilone and Pittsburgh's Omar Moreno, all speedsters, are among today's leading leg hitters.

# light ball

n: a ball thrown in such a manner and with a degree of spin that it feels light and easy as the player catches it. A pitch may be thrown at 100 mph and still feel light to the catcher. Nolan Ryan, Ron Guidry, and Tom Seaver, among many others, throw light balls.

*Ron Guidry*

*Gaylord Perry*

# load

vt: a euphemism that means to apply an illegal foreign substance, usually wet, to the ball. A pitcher suspected of throwing a spitball is said to be "loading 'em up." "If he's loading 'em up, the ball will sink," shortstop Fred Patek said of Gaylord Perry, considered baseball's leading spitball practitioner.

# location

n: the accuracy of a pitch. Location is used as a measure of a pitcher's control, i.e. "good location" and "bad location." Location and velocity are stilted terms used frequently in the evaluation of a pitcher (see velocity).

*Juan Marichal*

# long reliever

n: a pitcher summoned from the bullpen early in the game and used in long relief stints.

(long reliever cont'd)

Also called a long man.

# long tater

**n:** a home run, an expression that began as "long potatoes" many years ago in the Negro leagues and was adopted by players everywhere as one of the game's most common slang terms. It was popularized in the late 60s by Boston's George Scott.

# lumber

**n:** a collective term for a lineup filled with good hitters or simply a collection of bats. A team may boast "a lot of lumber" or a hitter breaking his bat may go back to the rack for "a new piece of lumber."

The "Lumber Company"
From left to right: Willie Stargell, Dave Parker, Al Oliver, Manny Sanguillen

# Magic number

**n:** a number that is the combination of wins and losses needed by the leading and second-place teams to ensure math-

(magic number cont'd)

ematical elimination of the second~place team from the pennant race. If the magic number is 10 and the leading team wins 10, the second team cannot win the pennant, even if it wins 10. If the second~place team loses five of its remaining games, then the leading team has only to win five of its games to make the magic number and win the pennant.

# meat hand

n: the player's throwing hand, as opposed to the one protected by the glove. A catcher's meat hand is highly vulnerable to injury.

# mop up

vi: to pitch in relief after the pitcher's team is hopelessly behind. The reliever is asked to complete the game or mop up the damage that already has been done. Good pitchers are rarely used for mopping up. A pitcher designated to mop up is known as the mop~up man.

# mound

n: a circular area, 18 feet in diameter and elevated by no more than 10 inches, containing a rubber plate, from which the pitcher delivers the ball to the hitter. A pitcher is sometimes known as a moundsman and a group of pitchers as the mound corps.

# move

n: a pitcher's technique in throwing to a base to pick off a runner. Because he faces first base as he winds up, a left~hander normally has a good move to first.

# mowing them down

vt: the ability of the pitcher to retire batter after batter.

# mustard

n: one of many heat~related designations for fastball. A good fastball has a lot of mustard on it.

*Don Mattingly*

# MVP

n: Most Valuable Player award, the most prestigious in base-ball. Every year, an MVP is picked from each league by a vote of the Baseball Writers of America. Two writers from each of the 26 major~league cities participate in the voting. Each writer votes for 10 players, starting with his No.1 choice at the top and completing the ballot in descending order. A first~place vote is worth 14 points, second~place nine points, third~place eight, fourth~place seven, fifth~place six, sixth~place five, seventh~place four, eighth~place three, ninth~place two and 10th~place one. The practice started in 1931.

# Nightcap

n: the second game of a double~header. The term originated because a nightcap is the final drink of the evening before retiring.

# Off the table

prep. phrase: a complimentary phrase reserved for especially good

Tommy
John

(off the table cont'd.)

sinking pitches--sinkers, forkballs
and spitballs. Tommy John, Mel
Stottlemyre, Catfish Hunter and
others who specialized in pitches
that appear to roll off the table, forced
batters to hit the ball on the ground.

# ohfer

n: a hitless day for a hitter, as in
"oh for three."

# on deck

prep. phrase: in position to be the
next hitter, derived from the nautical expression to be on
deck and ready. The hitter to follow the man on deck is "in
the hole," which may come from "hold," a nautical term
that means the interior of a ship. In a measure designed to
help speed up the game, baseball in the 1960s adopted a
rule requiring a batter to be on deck.

# open stance

n: the positioning of the batter's feet in which his front
foot is farther away from the plate than his back foot. The
front foot, however, is not far enough away to qualify for being
in the bucket (see foot in bucket.)

# out man

n: a weak hitter, one generally regarded as likely to make
an out. The worst hitter statistically among established (at
least 2,500 at-bats) non-pitchers was Bill Bergen, a catcher
for Cincinnati and Brooklyn in the early 1900s. In 947 games,

(out man cont'd.)

Bergen batted .170. Two of the most notoriously bad~hitting pitchers were Bob Buhl of the Braves and Cubs and Sandy Koufax of the Dodgers. Buhl batted .089 in 857 at~bats and Koufax .097 in 776 at~bats.

# out pitch

n: the pitcher's favorite, the one he depends upon to get an out.

# Parachute

n: one of many designations for a softly hit pop fly that flutters just beyond the reach of the infielders and abruptly descends to earth, landing just in front of the on~rushing outfielders. Also known as a quail shot, wounded duck and Texas League single. To the baseball purist, a wounded duck and a quail shot do not gain as much altitude as a parachute.

# park

vt: to hit a home run, as in "he parked one."

Babe Ruth

# payoff pitch

n: when there is a full count, that is, three balls and two strikes, the next pitch must pay off (if not fouled off) in a walk, a strikeout, or a ball in fair play.

# peg

n: a throw, especially one from an outfielder.

# Peggy Lee fastball

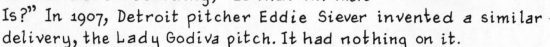

n: a self~effacing remark describing a fastball, authored by the Phillies' Tug McGraw several years ago. It's an allusion to Miss Lee's recording, "Is That All There Is?" In 1907, Detroit pitcher Eddie Siever invented a similar delivery, the Lady Godiva pitch. It had nothing on it.

# pepper

n: a traditional pre~game ritual in which a player, standing at close range, makes a short, quick throw to another player, who uses a bat to punch the ball crisply to the players directly in front of him. The player fielding the ball tosses it back quickly to the batter and the pepper game continues along at a fast pace.

# phantom double play

n: a double play in which the out at second base is only an illusion, or a phantom. The infielder--either the shortstop or second baseman--takes the throw from another infielder, moves quickly across the bag without touching it, eludes the sliding runner and throws to first to complete the play. Umpires are aware of this rules violation but continue to ignore it as long as the throw to second base beats the runner. If the runner is safe at first, the name changes to phantom force play.

# phenom

(pronounced fē-näm) n: a rookie with extraordinary credentials or one who opens the season spectacularly, thus earning

Kent Hrbek

(phenom cont'd.)

himself a reputation as being a phenomenal player. Phenoms, however, often fade quickly. The term was coined by sports writer Garry Schumacher and first applied to the Giants' Clint Hartung, who in the spring of 1947 was considered an outstanding pitcher~outfielder, a combination of Walter Johnson and Mel Ott, it was said. But he developed into nothing more than a mediocre player. Early in the 1982 season, New York Times columnist Dave Anderson described Minnesota's Kent Hrbek as a phenom. Hrbek led the league in homers and RBIs after the first month of the season and continued to rank among the top three in those departments through mid~June. He finished the season with a .301 batting average, 23 home runs and 93 RBIs.

# pick it

**vt**: to pick up or field a ground ball, especially one that is difficult to handle. A mid~70s term, it is generally used as an exhortation among teammates. A ground ball in the direction of the shortstop may elicit shouts of "Pick it" from teammates. If the shortstop succeeds in making the play, he is likely to hear his teammates compliment him by saying, "Way to pick." In discussing an infielder adept at fielding ground balls, ballplayers often say, "He can pick it."

Ozzie Smith

# pickoff

n: a play involving a runner on base in which either the pitcher or catcher suddenly throws to a teammate with the intent of catching the runner off base and tagging him out. Signals between the pitcher, catcher and infielders are often used to set up a pickoff.

# pill

n: a good fastball, one that approaches the plate so rapidly that to the batter it looks as small as a pill.

# pitchout

n: a ball deliberately pitched at least a foot wide of the plate so that the batter cannot hit it and the catcher can move into ideal position for throwing out the runner. A pitchout is called, usually by the catcher or manager, if there is a suspicion that a base runner will attempt to steal.

Warren
Spahn

# portsider

n: a left~hander. Port denotes the left~hand side of a ship.

# power alleys

n: the left~center and right~center field areas where strong hitters are capable of hitting for their greatest distances.

# pull

**vt**: to hit the ball early (the bat meets the ball in front of the batter) and thereby generate maximum power. A right~hand hitter pulls the ball to the left side and vice~versa. Pull hitters often produce high home run totals but low batting averages. A notable exception was Ted Williams, a pull hitter who hit 521 homers and batted .344.

*Ted Williams*

# pull the string

**vt**: to throw a pitch with significantly less velocity with the hope of fooling the batter who may be expecting a fast one. Such a pitch is known as a change~up or off~speed pitch.

# punch

**n**: the ability to produce plenty of hits and runs. A good~hitting team has a lot of punch in the lineup.

# Punch~and~Judy hitter

**n**: a hitter who specializes in softly hit but well~placed singles. Pete Rose, a noted singles hitter, has described himself as a "Judy hitter."

*Pete Rose*

# punchout

**n**: a strikeout, derived from the act in which a boxer punches out his opponent. A pitcher who strikes

(punchout cont'd.)

out a big hitter in a clutch situation may later boast that "I punched him out."

# purpose pitch

n: a pitch whose purpose is to back the batter away from the plate. The late Branch Rickey, one of the game's greatest executives and innovators, once said, "That was a purpose pitch, the purpose being to separate the batter's head from his shoulders."

# Quail shot

n: also dying quail, a base hit that resembles the flight of a quail-- a modestly hit pop fly that falls quickly to earth between the outfielders and infielders. Former Pittsburgh centerfielder Bill Virdon seemed to specialize in such hitting and was nicknamed the Quail.

# Rabbit ears

n: a label applied to players or umpires who are especially sensitive to criticism or taunts that are shouted at them while they're on the field. They seem to hear everything. Umpires are most frequently the target of verbal abuse and are frequently said to have rabbit ears.

# radio ball

n: a pitch that goes by so fast that

(radio ball cont'd)

the hitter hears it but doesn't see it.

# rain check

**n:** a detachable portion of a ticket that entitles the holder in the event of a rainout to admission to another game. Rain checks were first used in New Orleans in 1888. The term has been adapted into general usage to mean the postponement of acceptance of an invitation, as in "I'll take a rain check."

# retread

**n:** a veteran player whose career seems at an end but who is given another chance with a new team.

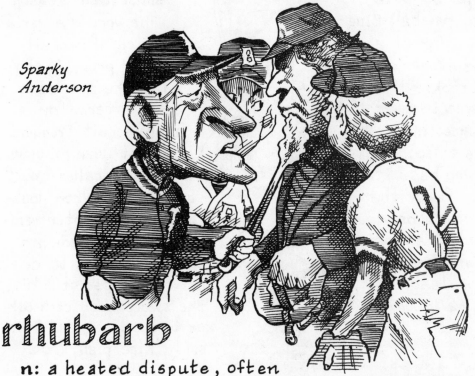

*Sparky Anderson*

# rhubarb

**n:** a heated dispute, often resulting in fisticuffs, involving many players from both teams. The term was popularized by Dodgers sportscaster Red Barber (see Barber profile).

# ribbies

n: a derivative of RBIs, a smooth~sounding, easily articulated alternative to the clumsy RBI.

# right down the pike

prep. phrase: an expression for a pitch that crosses the center of the strike zone. Because such a pitch is inviting to the hitter, a skillful pitcher tries to avoid it.

# rookie

n: a first~year player or one who has played so sparingly in a previous season that he still meets the Baseball Blue Book's definition of a rookie. A non~pitcher qualifies as a rookie if he has appeared in fewer than 30 games in a previous season. A pitcher who has appeared in fewer than 60 innings in a previous season is still a rookie. A player who has been on a major~league

*Wally Joyner*

roster for at least 90 days does not qualify as a rookie in a subsequent season.

The word is a variation of recruit and probably started in the army as a derisive term for a fresh recruit. Frequently, first~year players are simply called "rook" by veterans. When Houston's rookie centerfielder Terry Puhl made an excellent catch to deprive Pete Rose of a hit, the two passed each other in the field, and Rose said, "Nice play, Rook."

# rotation

n: the sequence in which a team's starting pitchers are scheduled to pitch.

# rubber

n: a rubber plate, 24 inches by 6 inches, which the pitcher's pivot foot must be touching as he releases the pitch. The rubber is located 60 feet, 6 inches from the rear point of home plate.

# run~and~hit

n: a play in which a runner on first breaks for second and the batter has the option to swing at the pitch but is not obligated to do so. On the hit~and~run, the runner breaks for second, and the hitter is obligated to make contact with the pitch and thereby tries to protect the runner from being thrown out. On a straight steal, the runner breaks and tries to advance to the next base without help or hindrance from the batter.

# Saw~off

vt: to pitch on the inside corner of the plate, forcing the hitter into the awkward position of having to hit the ball with the handle of the bat. Such a pitch seems to "saw off" the barrel of the bat.

# scatter arm

n: a pitcher or fielder prone to pitching or throwing the ball wildly, thereby scattering it all over the field.

# screaming meemie

n: a menacing low line drive that hisses, or screams, as it

(screaming meemie cont'd.)

flies through the air. The term was first applied to German artillery shells in World War II and later adapted to baseball.

Fernando Valenzuela

# scroogie

n: derivative of screwball, a pitch that has a reverse spin and breaks in the opposite direction to a curve ball.

# send

vt: to order a base~runner to advance to the next base, usually on the next pitch. Coaches and managers are often exhorted by the fans to "send him."

# seventh~inning stretch

n: the period at the beginning of each half of the seventh inning when fans of the team coming to bat stand up and stretch. It is probably

(seventh~inning stretch)

as old as baseball itself. A player who made note of the seventh~ inning stretch was Harry Wright of the Cincinnati Red Stockings, who in 1869 wrote to a friend: "The spectators all arise between halves of the seventh inning, extend their legs and arms and some- times walk about." Another story related to its origin is that President Taft, attending a game in Washington, stood up in the middle of the seventh, and the fans, thinking he was leaving, stood in deference to the President.

# shell

   **n:** usually used as a word that describes the fact that oppos- ing batters got many hits off the pitcher. "He got shelled" is ap- plied to the pitcher who permitted an excessive number of rockets, or hard~hit balls."

# shoestring catch

   **n:** a running catch, usually by an outfielder, made close to the tops of his shoes.

# short fuse

   **n:** a quick reaction by an umpire to throw a player out of the game when the ump's de- cision is challenged. An umpire with a short fuse is one who, hearing only a few dissenting words from a player who dis- putes a call, explodes with an animated "out" gesture that signifies the dissenter has been banished.

*Bill Klem*

# short porch

n: a home run barrier in right or left field that is a shorter distance from home plate than in most ballparks. The term probably originated because of the design of many of the old parks. The seats surrounding the outfield were covered by a roof and resembled a porch.

# short reliever

n: a pitcher who specializes in late~inning relief, that is, he pitches only a few innings, and who sometimes is called on for these short stints three and four days in a row. Also known as a short man

# sit on

vt: to wait for or anticipate a specific pitch. Aware that a pitcher depends on his fastball when he's behind in the count, a smart hitter will "sit on the fastball" and be able to give it a ride. "I was sittin' on the fastball" is common clubhouse talk.

Earl Weaver

# sittin' duck

n: a base~runner who foolishly tries to advance or steal but is out by a wide margin. He thereby is a sitting duck easier to shoot for the fielder making the throw.

# sitting in the catbird seat

vt: sitting pretty. Former Dodgers sportscaster Red Barber picked it up from an opponent in a poker game and popularized it.

# skipper

n: an affectionate term for manager. Players sometimes address the manager as "Skip."

# slap hitter

**n:** one who slaps, rather than swings, at the ball with the intent of punching it just over the infielders' heads. Schooled by Harry Walker in the fine art of slap hitting, Pittsburgh's Matty Alou won a batting title in 1966 with a .342 average. Of his 183 hits, 154 were singles.

# slice

**n:** a ball that is hit in such a manner that it spins excessively and curves, depending on whether it was hit by a right~ or left~ hander. A slice by a right~hand hitter curves to the right. For a left~hander, it curves to the left.

*Matty Alou*

# smoke

**n:** a good fastball, one that figuratively smokes because of all the friction it generates. Also used as a verb--"Smoke him." In his book BALL FOUR, Jim Bouton writes that a favorite piece of advice offered by Seattle Pilots pitching coach Sal Maglie was "Smoke him inside."

# solo homer

**n:** a home run with no one on base.

# sophomore jinx

**n:** bad luck that befalls a second~year player who was outstanding in his rookie season. One of the best examples is Cleveland's Joe Charboneau, who was named

*Joe Charboneau*

(sophomore jinx cont'd)

The Sporting News Rookie of the Year in 1980 and who was the subject of a book and a song. He was given the nickname Super Joe. But in 1981, he slumped, partly because of a back injury, and was demoted for two weeks to the Charleston (W.Va.) Charlies. Because he didn't expect to remain in Charleston long, he slept on a couch in Manager Frank Lucchesi's office. Another sophomore jinx victim was Walt Dropo of the Boston Red Sox, who batted .322 with 34 home runs and 144 RBIs to win rookie of the year honors in 1950. In 1951, however, he hit .239 with 11 homers and 57 RBIs.

Sandy Koufax

# southpaw

n: a left~hander, usually a pitcher. At one time, ballparks were laid out with home plate to the west, meaning that a left~handed pitcher faced the south. The word was originated by Finley Peter Dunne, a sports writer for the Chicago News and a former associate of Ring Lardner. Dunne and Charles Seymour of the Chicago Herald were using "southpaw" as early as 1887. Dunne and Seymour also are credited with the modern style of baseball writing in which they emphasized the game's most dramatic moments.

Bill Lee

# space cadet

n: a player who acts or talks nonsensically or eccentrically, as though he were from outer space. Pitcher Bill Lee is the premiere space cadet of the present but is no match for Herman (Germany) Schaefer, the Detroit second baseman of the Ty Cobb era. Schaefer once stole first base, probably the only player in history to do so. In a game against Cleveland in 1908, he was on first and Davey Jones on third. When the sign was flashed for the double steal, Schaefer stole second, but Jones chose to stay at third. Schaefer then yelled, "Let's try it again," and on the next pitch raced back to first. He promptly stole second again, unnerving the pitcher and enabling Jones to score from third. On another occasion, he strode to the plate, turned to the crowd and, in glowing terms, informed the fans of his presence.

# spitball

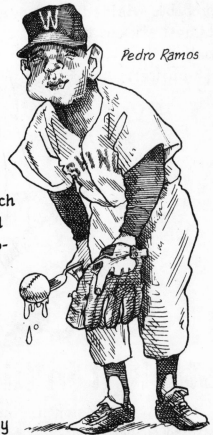

Pedro Ramos

n: a pitch in which the pitcher uses a foreign substance to wet the ball to give it an erratic motion. It was banned in 1920 but still is practiced on the sly by a few of today's hurlers. A well~thrown spitball sinks abruptly and is sometimes known euphemistically as a super sinker. The pitch is also called a spitter, Vaseline pitch and pine tar ball, depending on the foreign substance the pitcher applies to the ball to cause it to react. Former Washington pitcher Pedro Ramos, a Cuba native and alleged spitball practitioner, called his pitch a Cuban forkball. If Ramos indeed did throw a spitball, he at least gave it a respectable name and doubtless chose to call it a forkball because it reacts similarly

(spitball cont'd)

to a spitter. When the pitch was outlawed, the rule stipulated that pitchers active in 1920 would be permitted to continue using the pitch for the duration of their careers. As a result, the last man to use the spitball legally was Burleigh Grimes, who retired in 1936.

# squeeze

n: a planned play, also known as the safety squeeze, in which the runner at third waits until the batter bunts the ball and then darts for the plate if he thinks he can make it safely. (See suicide squeeze)

# stick

n: a bat or a hitter. Hitters are often classified as good sticks and weak sticks. Babe Ruth probably wielded the largest stick in baseball history--a 48-ouncer.

*Babe Ruth*

# stick it in his ear

vt: an expression urging the pitcher to throw the ball there, favored by bench jockeys to unnerve the opposing hitter.

# stopper

**n:** an outstanding starting pitcher who can be counted on to pitch a winning game and stop a losing streak.

*Ty Cobb*

# strawberry

**n:** a strawberry~like abrasion usually on the hip or leg caused by sliding. Ty Cobb alleviated the problem by wearing sliding pads.

# stuff

**n:** a pitcher's assortment of effective pitches for a given game. Stuff is a commodity that is constantly being evaluated. A pitcher may say, "I had good stuff," or, "I didn't have good stuff."

# suicide squeeze

**n:** a planned play in which the base~ runner on third breaks with the pitch, as if he were trying to steal home. At the same time, the batter tries to execute a successful bunt, enabling the runner to score. If the batter fails to bunt, the runner is an easy out, a suicide. A suicide squeeze is never attempted with two out because a bunt usually results in the batter being thrown out at first.

# swinging bunt

**n:** a contradiction of terms that applies to a batted ball that rolls perhaps 30 feet. The hitter may have taken a mighty swing, perhaps thinking of hitting a home run, but made very little contact. Swinging bunts often result in base hits.

# Take him deep

**vt**: to hit a home run. A late 70s expression, it is sometimes used by pitchers victimized by home run hitters. Upon his demotion to Charleston (International League) following a two~week stint with the parent Houston Astros in 1979, pitcher Gary Wilson was recounting his experiences and said, "Jack Clark took me deep."

# take something off of it

**vt**: to throw a pitch with less velocity than previous pitches to upset the batter's timing. It may be an off~speed pitch or a change~up.

# tape~ measure homer

**n**: an extraordinarily long home run. Babe Ruth once hit one that cleared the roof at what is now Tiger Stadium and supposedly traveled 620 feet. Mickey Mantle hit a 565~foot shot at Griffith Stadium. Cincinnati's Ernie Lombardi hit a home run at Crosley Field that traveled 30 miles. It was a routine homer that landed in a moving truck.

# Texas League single

**n**: a ball lofted weakly into the shallow outfield that drops in for a hit just out of the reach of infielders and outfielders. Such hits were common in Texas in the late 1880s. Art Sunday, a former Texas League player, got a few of these upon being acquired by Toledo of the International League in about 1890. A local sports writer wrote that he had delivered "another of those Texas League hits" and the term gained acceptance.

# tools

**n**: physical skills needed to play baseball. "The kid's got all the tools," Dodger third baseman Ron Cey said of young Steve Sax, the

(tools cont'd)

team's new second baseman. For many years, baseball skills have been divided into five areas: hitting, hitting for power, running, throwing and fielding. Rarely does a player excel in all five. Two notable exceptions have been Hall of Famers Joe DiMaggio and Willie Mays.

Joe DiMaggio

# tools of ignorance

**n**: the catcher's equipment. The implication is that only a stupid man would undertake such a hazardous position. The term was coined by catcher Muddy Ruel, who played for the Washington Senators in the 1920s and was a lawyer in the off~season.

Yogi Berra

# 'tweener

**n**: a sharply hit ball that drops between the outfielders and usually rolls to the fence for extra bases. The term, however, doesn't apply to a ball hit between two infielders.

# twin killing

**n**: a double play.

# Uncle Charlie

**n**: an outstanding curve ball.

# Velocity

n: the speed of a pitch. Velocity and location are often used in tandem in the assessment of pitchers. A pitcher with good velocity and good location is able to throw hard to a pre~determined spot. Pitchers themselves speak in those terms to the media in post~game evaluations of their performances. In an earlier era, pitchers simply threw hard and had good control; now they have good velocity and location. Comparisons of a pitcher's velocity are often made in distances, rather than miles per hour. A pitcher who is not as fast as he once was may have "lost a yard off his fastball," meaning the pitch is still a yard away from the plate in the time it formerly took to reach it.

Roberto Clemente

# Went the other way

vi: to have hit to the side of the field, either left or right, that is away from the hitter's natural strength. A right~hander's strength is to left; a hit to the right, therefore, is an opposite~field hit. The batter is said to have gone the other way.

Roberto Clemente, with 3000 hits and a .317 lifetime batting average, often **went the other way.**

# wheelhouse

n: the area of the strike zone in which the hitter delights in seeing the ball pitched -- usually waist~high and across the center of the plate. A pitcher fretting a home run may say, "I got it up in his wheelhouse."

# wheels

n: a player's legs. A fast runner has good wheels. A slow runner

(wheels cont'd.)

or one with chronic leg trouble has bad wheels. A player who incurs a leg injury has a bad wheel.

# whiff

**n, vi:** a strikeout or to strike out, derived from the whiff of air produced by the swing of the bat.

Walter Johnson

# whitewash

**n:** a shutout. The Chicago Cubs pitchers of the early 1900s combined for so many whitewashings that the term "Chicagoed" became synonymous with being shut out. Walter Johnson is the all~time whitewash leader with 113.

# wood

n: the amount of contact between the bat and a pitch. A good hitter is one who consistently gets, "a lot of wood on the ball."

# worm~burner

n: a ground ball that, because of heavy top~spin, rolls briskly across the infield without bouncing.

# wounded duck

n: a short, weakly hit fly ball that descends suddenly to the ground between the outfielders and infielders in the manner of a duck plummeting to earth after being hit by a hunter's bullet.

# Yakker

n: a sharp~breaking curve. An old term, it was probably named for the bird, yawker, a type of woodpecker whose undulating flight resembles the path of a curve.

# yellow hammer

n: another long~standing term for a sharp~breaking curve that apparently was also named for a bird, the yellowhammer, a woodpecker (the yellow~shafted flicker) that dips abruptly in flight.

# NICKNAMES

Without nicknames, many of baseball's greatest names would be barely recognizable to generations of fans. George Ruth, Lynwood Rowe, Harold Traynor, Lawrence Berra, Jim Grant, and Jim Hunter hardly evoke the nostalgia of Babe, Schoolboy, Pie, Yogi, Mudcat, and Catfish. Almost without exception, the game's most famous nicknames were born of impulse ~~ usually by a childhood friend or teammate ~~ and will be forever a part of the baseball lexicon.

## Lawrence Peter (YOGI) Berra.

Larry Berra became Yogi Berra at a movie theater as a youngster growing up in St. Louis. He and his friends were watching a travelogue about India in which one of the people was a Hindu fakir who was called a yogi. Jack Maguire, who later played shortstop for the New York Giants, thought the yogi resembled Berra and said, "I'm gonna call you Yogi."

The "Can"

## Dennis (OIL CAN) Boyd.

In his hometown of Meridian, Miss., oil was a part of black dialect that meant beer. A friend noted that young Dennis Boyd always seemed to be holding an oil can.

## Joe (YANKEE CLIPPER) DiMaggio.

A swift New York-to-Boston train known as the Yankee Clipper was the inspiration for DiMaggio's nickname. It was coined by Yankee announcer Arch McDonald. In 1941, a song, "Joltin' Joe DiMaggio," was written in his honor and thus gave rise to another nickname.

## Mark (THE BIRD) Fidrych.

His frizzy hair, long legs and loping stride reminded teammates of Big Bird, the character on *Sesame Street*.

## Lou (IRON HORSE) Gehrig.

The Yankee first baseman set a major-league record by playing in 2,130 consecutive games and thus was named for a powerful and durable locomotive.

## Jim (MUDCAT) Grant.

A teammate, mistakenly thinking Grant hailed from Mississippi, the Mudcat State, began calling him "Mudcat." Grant, however, was a native of Florida.

## Charles (GABBY) Hartnett.

He was so shy as a rookie with the Cubs in 1922 that teammates sarcastically called him "Gabby." Another quiet player, the Dodgers' John Roseboro, was sometimes called Gabby.

*"The Iron Horse"*

## Jim (CATFISH) Hunter.

Although an avid fisherman, Hunter did not acquire his nickname because of an incident involving catfish. Kansas City owner Charles Finley, after signing Hunter to a contract in 1964, gave him the nickname on the spot. It was typical of Finley's penchant for promotional gimmickry.

## Reggie (MR. OCTOBER) Jackson.

The name began appearing in the media as Jackson continually excelled in the playoffs and World Series.

## Walter (BIG TRAIN) Johnson.

Sports writer Grantland Rice, grasping for a nickname worthy of Johnson's awesome pitching skills, wrote in 1911: "The Big Train comes to town today." It was an era in which nicknames were standard fare for the game's best players.

### Willie (THE SAY HEY KID) Mays.

Overwhelmed by media attention and new faces in the early weeks of his career in 1951, a bewildered Mays developed the habit of saying, "Say who?", "Say what?", and "Say hey!" New York sports writer Barney Kremenko began calling him the Say Hey Kid and Giants announcer Russ Hodges promoted the nickname on his broadcasts.

### Wilmer (VINEGAR BEND) Mizell.

Mizell was a native of Vinegar Bend, Alabama.

*"The Man"*

### Stan (THE MAN) Musial.

"Here comes that man again," said the fans at Brooklyn's Ebbets Field. Musial, a lifetime .333 hitter, hit especially well in the Dodgers' tiny ballpark.

### John (BLUE MOON) Odom.

His boyhood friends nicknamed him "Moon" because of his moon-shaped face. Later, his professional teammates embellished the nickname to "Blue Moon" because he often appeared downcast.

### Dave (THE COBRA) Parker.

His coiled batting stance reminded Pirate announcer Bob Prince of a cobra.

### Phil (THE SCOOTER) Rizzuto.

The 5-foot-6 Rizzuto seemed to scoot after ground balls and was nicknamed the Scooter by teammates in a New York amateur league.

### Pete (CHARLIE HUSTLE) Rose.

As a rookie with the Reds in 1963, Rose drew a base on balls in an exhibition game against the Yankees. Typically, he sprinted to first base, prompting Mickey Mantle to ask: "Who's that Charlie Hustle?"

### Lynwood (SCHOOLBOY) Rowe.

Once known as "Newsboy," Rowe acquired his nickname in his early years while pitching in El Dorado, Ark. "Don't let that schoolboy strike you out," the fans said to the batters.

### George Herman (BABE) Ruth.

As a 19-year-old, Ruth signed his first professional contract to play for the Baltimore Orioles of the International League. The Orioles' manager, Jack Dunn, was noted for signing young players. When Ruth, accompanied by Dunn, first arrived, one of the veterans said, "Here comes Dunn and another one of his babes." While with the Yankees, Ruth acquired another famous nickname—Bambino, which means "babe" in Italian.

## Willie (POPS) Stargell.
In 1979 at age 38, Stargell began referring to himself as "Pops" when he led the Pirates to a world championship.

## Harold (PIE) Traynor.
One of his boyhood chores was going to the grocery store for his mother, carrying a list she had given him. In reading the list to the grocer, he invariably ended with "and one pie." The grocer's son, a baseball companion, began calling him "Pie."

"Pie"

# INDEX